The Face of Expression 3

Fall of a King

Aaron Woodson

The Face of Expression 3: Fall of a King
Copyright © January 2023 Aaron Woodson
ISBN# 978-1-953526-32-8

Published by TaylorMade Publishing
Jacksonville, FL
www.TaylorMadePublishingFL.com
(904) 323-1334

TaylorMade Publishing

TABLE OF CONTENTS

Introduction

Aaron Woodson was born on May 6th, 1983, in his hometown of Vallejo, California. He currently lives in Jacksonville, Florida. He is a former U.S. Air Force military veteran, published author, poet, narrator, screenplay writer, actor, dancer, and artist.

This book is his highly anticipated poetry release called THE FACE OF EXPRESSION 3: FALL OF A KING. It's the 3rd and final installment in the trilogy series. Readers will enjoy a variety of new, exciting, eclectic, and gripping poetry like they have never experienced before!

Journey through a therapeutic experience of love, victory, adversity, courage, healing, spirituality, growth, adventure, and unapologetic honesty. Written from a man with heart of a lion, all while leaving his mark on this world! Enjoy this latest masterpiece!!

Chess With God

(*Quan Zanders*)
From the time you enter the world
there is a pulling…a tugging at your soul.
Constantly bombarded with images and sounds
that try to make you see, hear, and think a certain away.

The board seems so small
as your opponent matches your move for move.
Crying out "Lord please help me I am trapped!"
You are all out of moves and are blocked on every side
when the entire time that still small voice replies,
"stand aside and let me provide."
Stand aside?... trust?

The concept seems so foreign so instead
we bargain in partial obedience.
"Well, if you will take care of this LORD
I can handle the rest."
Checkmate…the strong man has fallen,
and chaos has made it into your camp.
"Will You just trust Me?"

(*Aaron Woodson*)
As we enter this maze called life.
We move through many areas and try to take up as
much space as we can. There is only one problem,
there is only so much we don't see…
so much we don't know.

We're familiar with the light and the darkness,
and that's because we've been on
both sides of each spectrum.
I can picture all of us being on a chess board

1

battling each other trying to win
the war for bragging rights.
Trying to win accolades, riches, admiration, power,
and control of everything and everyone around us.
But what if we all had an opponent
that we were absolutely no match for?

There is a saying, "that for every level,
there is a different devil."
Yet ironically, in this game of chess,
there are no devils.
It's just between YOU and GOD!

We try to impose our will and
have it our own way…
But God chuckles to Himself
and let us think we may have gotten the better of Him.
Suddenly, He makes a move
that we didn't see coming
or were not expecting.

He blocks off access to what we think is good for us.
He presents obstacles not to harm us,
but to build up our character and
strengthen our faith in Him.
God wants us to realize that
we can't do anything without Him or
without Him knowing.

He also wants to let us know
that He knows all things and
that He is the King of all Kings
and the Lord of all Lords.
He humbles us and teaches us
the rules of the game
because He loves us so much!

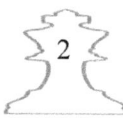

God knows all our moves.
He is always more than one step ahead of us.
He shows us the way.

He moves us in the direction He wants us to go.
When we have nowhere else to go,
it's in our best interest to submit because
He's got us all in CHECKMATE!
It's time to stop playing Chess with God.

Leading With Love

Lead with love! Love comes with risk and
you may even bleed love like Jesus did on the cross!
Fear not! No greater love have we ever known.
Love came off the throne and touched the world.
Love walked into our lives as a guest of honor.

Love was an ambassador.
Love was and is a King.
Love didn't ride in on a white horse,
instead it rode in on a donkey.
This kind of love that we often speak of,
think of, and dream of swept nations off its feet.
Love has never been a tyrant,
but it has always ruled for generations.
Love is transcendent and we are blessed to be
its divine descendants.

We've all played the fool,
maybe some of us are still acting like a fool...
but love still loves a fool!
Love wants to make the foolish wise.
Love wants to open our eyes.
Love wants us to open our hearts.
Love wants us to open our hands.
Love even wants us to open our mouths to praise!
Love always knew how to raise its children.
Love is a bond that grows beyond a lifetime.
Love breaks barriers.
It heals. It feels.
And it understands what we may be going through.
Love is our neighbor.

Love should be welcome as our gracious visitor and friend.

Love bears fruit, that nourishes our soul.
Love values and protects.
Love penetrates what is hardened.
Love fills the cracks. Love fills the void.
Love is gentle. Love is kind. Love forgives.
Love is enough. Love doesn't quit.
Love admits, but it also knows how to submit.
Love is undefeated. Love is a soldier on the front lines.
Love doesn't keep score. Love goes to war
but it always remains victorious. Love prevails.

Love unveils the truth. Love is a shield of faith.
Love fights until the end. Love is a companion.
Love doesn't destroy, it builds. Love sits with the broken.
Love serves. Love appreciates. Love is pleasing and stimulating.
Love is passion. Love is a master of affection.
Love has no legislation. Love can't be regulated.
Love rejoices. Love always chooses. Love is clever.
Love is intimate. Love is a gift. Love is the answer.
Love is the way. Love is a miracle. Love is awesome.
Love is amazing. Love is special. Love is supportive.
Love is courageous.

Love is brilliant. Love is worth it.
Love will make you cry tears of joy.
Love makes the heart grow fonder. Love wonders.
Love is more than capable. Love is powerful. Love is majestic.
Love is a force. Love has the advantage over hate.
Love is a difference maker.
Love is not bound by anything or anyone.
Love is a promise. Love doesn't stop. Love ages well.
Love smiles. Love manifests.

Love prays. Love seeks. Love goes above and beyond.
Love expresses. Love is real and nothing about it is fake.
Love is sexy. Love is fun.

Love brings out the best in everyone. Love matters.
Love shines. Love endures. Love overcomes trials.
Love lives here! Love will never go away, it's here to stay.
And if no one else will love you,
well damn it, I'll love you! I mean it too!!

The Social Complex

Every term I hear these days has something to do with being social.
Manners were the normal practice at the dinner table
in some family homes a long time ago.
Then we became more social by going out to celebrate and
having a good time at social events with friends or
complete strangers we didn't even know.
Music, alcohol, dance moves, games, and even drugs
were introduced at these so called "hot spots."

We went from the era of house parties to bars and clubs.
Sometimes things got out of control when a
large group of people caused a ruckus.
The neighbors would often make such a fuss.
Sometimes all over nothing.
They probably just wanted to hate and
shut the party down by calling the police.
I get it we may have disturbed the peace,
but in our minds, we were just living our best lives.

As we are aware, some things just don't mix.
Attitudes, alcohol, drugs, and crowds don't always mix.
So, it was always important we would watch what we would say
and watch each other's backs.

Sometimes we would just have family functions and
just vibe with one another.
We had cookouts at the park or in the backyard.
We just wanted to have a funky good time.
But as time passed,
you noticed more separation and isolation.
People started to become busier and
live inside their own little "bubble."
What was once seen as unity and embracing

has now become abandonment and withdrawal.

Walls started going up as quickly as construction sites
around each block of the city.
As a military veteran,
I remember going to basic training in San Antonio, Texas and
my drill instructor would tell the flight group that
they would "tear us down and slowly build us back up!"
Well, that is how things have happened in each decade.
There is a time for everything under the sun.
A time to gather and a time to scatter.
Hearts grew cold and become became shattered pieces.

Life happens to us all and it hits hard like a fist.
Like Mike Tyson, once said, everyone has a plan
until they get hit in the face.
But in this case, most of us have taken some blows
to the body, the mind, heart, and in our pockets.
Pain can often leave you crippled or disabled if you allow it to.
We must heal from ourselves by removing toxic
behaviors, substances, and people out of our lives.
Being alone can feel like the most dangerous
place or position to be in.
But under the same breath
it can be a good sigh of relief momentarily.

I say all this to say, we started out being all in this together to become
digitally connected through social media. Technology has become the
substitute of human interaction.

Believe it or not, technology monitors our social activity on the
Internet. Social Media became a big phenomenon in the late 90's-early
2000's era. There were upsides and downsides to it.

Now, we have been confronted with a strange new intruder
by the name COVID-19.

It's a disease that has taken the world by storm and
has resulted in the government shutting down
our cities across the United States.
We are told by elected officials that we should
consider "social distancing."
That means you must wear a mask and
limit physical interaction with anyone others.
You, We now must be a safe distance of 6 ft
from talking to each other anyone.
Human Interactions have now changed
drastically at an alarming rate.
Some people are nervously awaiting their fate
at the hands of this pandemic.

Life as we know it will never be the same.
Some people are dealing with mental health issues,
depression, and social anxiety.

There is strength in numbers, but when the population's movement is
controlled, there is less social activity and gatherings.
There is a need for us all to be social,
we were created to desire friendships and relationships.

Going forward this will be a challenge
for us all in the foreseeable future.
Somehow, I believe we will overcome all this...
we will rise above this so-called
Social Complex that we are living in right now.

Grace

As we gather around the table
it is customary to say the blessing or say grace!
With our heads bowed and eyes closed, we honor
the food that has been prepared and offer thanksgiving!
It is to show reverence and remember that God
provided the meal, not anyone or anything else.

It is by the grace of God that we woke up this morning.
It's by the grace of God that we can still breathe.
It's by the grace of God that we can live in freedom
and not in the yoke of bondage.
There is just something amazing about the word Grace!
God's love is the gift of this amazing grace!
We did absolutely nothing to deserve this precious
Grace that we received.
Grace is the goodness of God!

How sweet the sound and that same grace
that saved a wretch like me.
We once were lost, but now we are found!
I once was blind, but now I see!
I really see because I have sought Your face.
Your glory is more than anyone can fathom.
It Is by your amazing grace that I can sing Your praises.
It is by your amazing grace that I can stand
firm on the foundations of my faith.

It is by Your amazing grace that I even have a hope and a future!
Thank you, Jesus! Thank you, Jesus! Thank you, Jesus!
I may have fallen out of favor with man or woman,
but I never fall out of favor or grace with You Lord.
You love me beyond my flaws and faults...
You never gave up on me!

You love every single person on this earth.
Your amazing grace is a true blessing.
I'm so grateful as we should all be!
Elvis created Graceland, but you created the whole universe
with Your miraculous power and grace.
Even when we fall, You're there to carry us through.
In my weakness, Your grace is more than sufficient.
Grace breaks through any barriers
that include race, gender, ethnicity, nationality,
origin, political affiliation, etc.
Grace is forgiving one another for their trespasses!
Grace and mercy abound!
I say to you my brothers and sisters,
go in peace and know that God's grace covers you.
He will never leave you nor forsake you.
Grace be unto you!

Your Labor is Not in Vain

My friend, your labor is not in vain.
Weeping may endure for a night,
but joy surely comes in the morning.
God is for you, and He is with you!

Through the good and bad times,
He is a constant friend.
In your weakness, His Grace is more than sufficient.
Though you may toil day and night, God sees you and
reminds you that in His timing you shall reap a harvest.
You planted the seed and tilled the ground,
but God will water your crop of blessing.
While you're waiting, praise God
for all that you have right now.
Be thankful and rejoice!

He didn't bring you this far to leave you now.
The Lord is near the brokenhearted and
saves those who are crushed in spirit. (Psalm 34:18)
In due time God will lift you up.
The vineyards you plant will bear fruit with you.
"Therefore, my dear brothers and sisters stand firm.
Let nothing move you.
Always give yourselves fully to the work of the Lord,
because you know that your labor in the Lord is not in vain."
(1 Corinthians 15:58)
My friend, be at peace and always remember that
your labor is not in vain! Amen!

Hello Handsome

Hello handsome
not sure if I told you this lately
but you are definitely handsome.
I haven't always felt or looked as handsome
but it's a blessing to appreciate who I really am.
God masterfully and carefully crafted Me by His design.
I am wonderfully and fearfully made
there is nobody in the world like me and
I take ownership of this handsome face
you all see before you.

God assign me the brilliant color
that represents everything about me.
He made me to be black I'm dark,
yet I am full of so much radiant light
nothing about me is blurred
what-you-see-is-what-you-get.

I can be a handful and then some.
My future love will be fortunate to have a man like me.
I'll tell her to come over here and
get you some of this sexual chocolate.
I know I'm smooth as cocoa butter and
I glow like the sun.
I'm sweet as a moon pie and
I'm refreshing like a good cup of coffee.
I'm a healthy young stallion that got big energy
my big smile reflects my wonderful personality.
I'm a powerful, bold charismatic,
eclectic, electric, passionate, phenomenal man.
I'm a handsome mighty man of God
I stand before you as a pillar,
but before I had to stand on the shoulders of giants.

I'm built for greatness
my eyes have vision to see beyond the surface.
I'm an imperfect person but made to make a difference.
I see a mountain of a man that is statuesque;
nothing about me is grotesque.

I don't need to hide my handsome face from anyone or anything.
It needs to reveal to the world God's extraordinary innovation.
I'm not ashamed to tell the world I'm handsome.
I got handsome sweating out of my pores
I don't mean to sound conceited; I just know my worth.
You can be humble,
but let's not forget to celebrate ourselves in the process.
Women love to be told that they are beautiful;
there is absolutely nothing wrong with being handsome.
I'll continue to be handsome for as long as I live and even if I die;
I'll forever be handsome because I was born and made that way.
So to all my fellas the next time you wake up
tell yourself hello handsome.

Balcony

As I'm sitting atop my hotel suite,
I enjoy the ambience and
fixtures that's around my presence.
There is a curtain in the far corner of the room and
behind it is a sliding glass door
that appears to be a window.
The translucent light peeks its way in
through the small opening of the curtain.
It hits my mahogany skin and
I feel the sun's radiant energy.

As I walk closer to welcome the sunshine,
I pull back the curtain and
reach for the glass door and
slide it all the way back.
In front of me, I see this elegant view
that captures my attention instantly.
It's breathtaking and draws me in.
As I walk even closer to the edge,
I noticed how high and
elevated I am from the ground.
I feel as though I can almost
touch the sky from where I am.

I feel like I've been in this scene before.
There is something nostalgic and
romantic about this place I recall being a balcony.
I've shared a few intense and
passionate romantic encounters
with someone here before!
This balcony has me reminiscing
about these bittersweet memories.

However, I also enjoy spending time all alone up here.
I'm free as a bird and I can see a whole new
world from my vantage point.
I can see the future. I can see the sun.
When the sun sets, I'll be able to see the moon and the stars.
I'm so used to being on solid ground
that it feels unstable for me to be at this position.
I'm starting to feel a little more adventurous lately,
but sometimes I'm afraid to jump.
Of course, not literally because that
would be stupid and total suicide.

I feel like I'm on top of a mountain from this balcony.
This is better than being in an elevator.
This feels like I've reached a climax,
but I don't want to come down from it at all.
I remember seeing movies with
the princess being at the top of the balcony
and a young Romeo trying to woo her!
I was that guy for sure!

To get to the top, you must climb
and go through some adversity.
I believe being on the balcony f
eels like you're on top of the world.
It's like the cherry on top, it's so exciting.
I feel like I'm a king and
I have ascended upon my balcony.
My balcony is my platform,
it's my safe place and it's my favorite place to stand and
watch over my surroundings.
I love my balcony!

Black By Popular Demand

I'm black as they come. I'm black as advertised.
I'm black by popular demand.
When I show up somewhere, I show up as BLACK!
Like Nas, I can go ultra-black...take it back to my roots.
Shout out to my Africans, Haitians, Dominicans,
Puerto Ricans, Jamaicans, and anywhere else ya'll from.

I'm permanent marker black like a sharpie
autographing my own books that I wrote.
I didn't need to cast a vote to be black!
I was already elected to be black!

To all my black kings and queens
we were made to be BLACK!
Walk in your distinction,
we are not going extinct anytime soon.
Blacks don't belong in no precinct.
Being black is not a crime.
Sometimes we do things we shouldn't do,
and we have to face consequences.
But sometimes our mere presence
gets us into trouble for no reason.

We belong at the table.
We are not waiting for anyone to give a seat;
we are making our own because now the tables have turned!!
You see, black has always been around and
it's not going away anytime soon.
I don't need any endorsements because of dark skin.
I'm valuable and know my worth.
I am a black man and a black king.
Hear my black conscience speaking to you.
I'm comfortable in my own damn skin!

Stop trying to say I sound white or
that I seem this way or that way.
God wonderfully and fearfully created me as
He did the same with the rest of us on this planet.
Let me remind you that I'm black as spade.
I always have an ace up my sleeve.
I will steal hearts and stay shining like these diamonds.

Being black can be tough
and sometimes a little rough
but I don't mind!
I wear my black with pride.
I know ya'll do too!
Black is bold. Black is beautiful.
Black in unique. Black is excellence.
Black is powerful! Black is deep.
Black is sexy. Black is authentic.
Black is real baby!!!

I'm happy being black and
if you're black you should be too!!
There is no shame in being black.
It's about time I spoke up for my black people.
Let's own our blackness and create more
opportunities for black businesses and entrepreneurship.
Black is globally recognized, so you can't cancel us!!

We are trendsetters and some real go-getters!
We are making a difference and
our impact is felt everywhere.
Our influence and culture are everywhere,
they can't stop us!
Black matters and it's here to stay!
Ya'll know ya'll love us!!
Don't be offended by the black narrative,
but it's imperative that we get our shine and just due.

We've broken barriers and paths
have been paved for me and my people to walk on.
We still got it going on.
So go on and tell us how great we are.
We already know that we got it like that,
and we will continue.
Ladies and gentlemen,
stay tuned for yet another season
of what I like to call
Black by Popular Demand!

A Run for Your Money

I'm not really interested in competing against anyone.
But one thing I will say is that
I'm not backing down from anyone
And I'll give anyone a run for their money!
I love a good challenge.
I'm not chasing any titles trophies or recognition.
I'm chasing God and the pursuit of greatness.

I have the heart of a champion and
I'm running this race called life.
I may not be the biggest, strongest, or
fastest guy in the world,
but I do have the biggest heart of a determination.
No one can stand a chance against my tenacity.
If I had to place a bet against me or someone else,

I'm picking me every time.
I don't have anything to lose.
I've made it this far in life and I'm still here.
I love my chances and I'm not afraid
to go after what I want.
I'm not afraid to use what I have either.
My money will be long as longevity.

I'm creating generational wealth
for me and my family.
I'm filling in those gaps,
won't be any lacking or slacking over here.
Like a marathon runner, I'm taking my victory lap!
Like Nipsey, I've been grinding all my life!
I'm a one-man tank capable of doing something groundbreaking.
You can even take that to the bank
cuz I'm giving all y'all a run for your money!

20

Pilot

Welcome aboard Flight 2022, my name is Aaron Woodson
and I'll be your pilot today.
We welcome you on this beautiful day traveling with us.
Any carry-on luggage you brought on today you can safely
stow away in the overhead bin or underneath your seat.
Please if you came on board with any drama,
please leave it at home.
We don't tolerate B.S. of any kind on this vessel.
We are topflight and a world class airline, okay!
Make sure you buckle your safety belt.
In case of an emergency, there are two exits on the side aisles
in the middle of this aircraft.
Your safety masks are in your overhead bin.
Before helping someone else with mask, we recommend you put
yours on first for your own safety.
Our estimated flight time of arrival to our destination
into Las Vegas will be 1:45pm.
You're in good hands with me and my assistant crew.
If you need anything just holla and
we'll make sure you're taken care of.

Now sit back and enjoy the ride.
I'm your pilot and I've got plenty of flying experience.
I've earned my wings and just so you know I'm a pretty fly guy!
The skies are friendly, but sometimes we encounter the storms of life.
You know what I'm saying.
You may feel a little bit of turbulence,
but we'll weather the storm together and level out.
I always believed I could fly and touch the sky.
I always believed I could soar.
Please ya'll, I don't wanna see you running through any open doors.
R. Kelly ("I Believe I Can Fly")
I think about it every night and day.

Watch me fly like an eagle, let this wind carry us.
I want fly...fly right into the future!
Seal ("Fly Like an Eagle")
I always dreamed of my baby flying me
to the moon like Frank Sinatra.
I would be more than happy to serenade her.
Cuz like Silk Sonic she knows that there is no one as fly as me!
I'm trying to love her, hoping that she loves me back!
Let's get back to basics, hope she takes a chance with me,
and I'll fly her across the world.
When we land, let's arrange for a private getaway
where it's just you and me!
I've earned my wings,
but I don't mind earning those stripes either baby!
So, tell me, did your pilot meet your satisfaction today?
Thank you for choosing Woodson Airlines and
look forward to having you travel
with me again soon!
Enjoy your stay!

Heart of A Lion

I love lions.
I'm always fascinated by these beautiful creatures.
Lions are menacing, fierce, regal,
bold, powerful, and confident.
Their distinctive roar will alarm anyone
in close range or from a distance.
They may not be the biggest, fastest,
or smartest animal in the world...
but they are the most courageous and
ferocious in the animal kingdom!
They are known as king of beasts!!
They have radiating eyes of gold
that pierce through any man or creatures' soul.
Their mouth houses razor sharp teeth
ready to tear into their unsuspecting prey.

Their mane shows off their cat daddy swag!
Their paws are pretty big, and their claw are very sharp!
I often thought of myself as a lion.
One thing no one really talks about is a lion's heart!
Lions will stop at nothing to go after what they want.
Lions are fearless and have a reputation for being the most
feared and respected creatures in the world.
Lions are not afraid of danger and are no strangers to it.
Lions have a dominating yet calm presence to them.

I'm lion-hearted because I've faced danger
on numerous occasions as an American soldier.
I was brave and my fellow soldiers were lion-hearted too!
We didn't back down and always looked for the next challenge.
We're not in the wild, but the world we know
we can become wild at any given moment.
Lions are champions and are natural leaders and protectors!

They are not shy to let anyone know whose boss!
I'm not afraid to let people know
I'm not one to mess with either.
I stand my ground and
I hunt for opportunities that present themselves to me.
Every one of us has a lion roaring on the inside of us.
Every now and then we need to let that lion roar!

Lions have pride and dignity.
They carry themselves like
they are on top of the food chain!
Don't be fooled by these big cats,
they don't play around!
Lions are not sheep.
They face opposition straight on and
don't cower or bow down to anyone!

Lions may have scars from battles they endure
but they continue to fight on.
In this life we all have our battles,
but these are battles we must fight.
Or better yet we have The Great Lion of Judah
that will come to our defense at any time!
God gave me a heart, but my heart is one of a kind.
I have the heart of a lion and that's perfectly fine!

Still on My Feet

I was hit by the unexpected.
I was surrounded by enemies
that were like sharks that smelled blood.
They attacked me relentlessly.
I held my own and stayed on my feet.

I didn't know how to accept defeat and
I sure wasn't about to retreat!
In the face of an ambush,
I fought back.
I kicked, scratched, and clawed
my way back to the top!
I will wear scars from the battles I've endured.
I got my head held high and
I've shaken everything off.
I'm still a king on the rise.
From sunrise to sunset each day,
I'll still be on my feet!

Rock Star

I'm a rock star not a pop star.
Never been a pop tart,
but my style is off the charts.
My art is a thing of beauty like Mozart.
Like Little Richard, I rock to the east.
I rock to the west!
I bounce to the north and
bounce to south.
C'mon let's rock!

I'm feeling a little bit nostalgic.
Don't make me go Elvis on ya'll!
Here's my impersonation.
"Uh-huh thank you very much!"
I'm a rocker that's been way off my rocker!
I can take you back to Woodstock like Jimi Hendrix!
Nothing I do is Betty Crocker.
So let me sock it to you like this.
I'm down to bring some of that heavy metal if I need to.
But I prefer to keep things nice and easy like Tina.

I even love to hit a few licks on my guitar like Santana.
I'm a soldier of love like Sade.
A rockstar is the life of the party.
What happens on stage stays on stage.
But behind the scenes is a different story.
Some people just like to kiss and tell.
Like Red Hot Chili Peppers, don't let me...
give it away, give it away, give it away now!
Show after show and tour after tour,
I always set it off and bring the house down!

When I find my old lady, she will dig my rock and
I will definitely dig her roll.
Sometimes when I want to go a little crazy,
I channel my inner Prince and say,
"Let's Go Crazy!" "Let's get nuts."
I'll switch it up on ya'll like Axl Rose
with his screaming guitar riff!
Or I'll play something like
"My Guitar Gently Weeps" by Clapton.
Like Queen, I've lived my own Bohemian Rhapsody.

Like Aerosmith, you gotta Dream On.
"Sing with me, sing for a year
Sing for the laughter, and sing the tear
Sing with me if it's just for today
Maybe tomorrow, the good Lord
will take you away."
Don't need a spliff, I get high off the Spirit.
I get high off this Rock N' Roll.
For me, Jesus Rocks and I Roll with Him!
I always said Jesus was a Rolling Stone!
He raised up from the dead and resurrected.

He is the King of all Kings.
He started the show, and He will make the grand finale!
I'm just a little rocker guy that found his way
and it led me to the ultimate encounter with my Savior!
God is the Greatest Rock Star
that transcends generations upon generations.
I'm just a blip on the radar, but while I'm here
I'm gonna keep rocking out while praising His name!
Thank you for being my Rock Jesus.
I roll with you for life.
I love you!

How To Be a Human

We are a species that has been created and
populated over all the face of the earth.
We are born and meant to exist beautifully as human beings!
We are also meant to coexist and inhabit the planet we live on.
As humans we have dominion and have been given the authority to

trample over serpents and scorpions.
We have access to vast and remarkable parts of the world.
We can speak many things into existence.
We are resilient creatures that can bounce back from almost anything.
Being human has acceptable and unacceptable behaviors.
We all have a responsibility to know the difference between
right and wrong or good and bad.

The human condition is fragile and complex.
Some of us want to flex and
act like we're so much better than someone else.
We as humans are nowhere near perfect,
but we're quite extraordinary people!
Humans have a capacity to feel deeply and
interact with our emotions.
There is not a recipe for being human,
but God's hands were at work for the creation to take place.
His Word was the ingredients that He used to make us.

The human spirit has an innate ability to survive its habitat!
It thrives in all sorts of different environments.
We can adapt and learn from our experiences or mistakes.
Most of us take risks, while others may not
be brave enough to take that initiative.
Humans have autonomy and free will to make
their own choices in life.
I believe to be human we need to understand what it's like to suffer.
Only in the suffering, we might be able to empathize with what

one another goes through in our personal lives.
Humans need order and healthy relationships to
understand the balance of this world.

I am a human that is unique and quite talented.
I have a big heart and kind spirit.
I feel for people and want to serve and help where I'm needed.
I'm flawed but I'm making progress by walking with God.
Humans all bleed the same and we all have a name.
Humans make the world a better place but sometimes we
cause destruction, confusion, pain, and despair!

Most humans like to fix things but sometimes
we're the ones in need of repairing.
One the best acts we can do as a human is to share and
care about each other.
Beyond that, we should assure to love each other,
and God loves us.
Love is the reason we are all here.
It is our responsibility for how we act as a human.
Being authentically you and living in peace and
harmony with others is how to be a human!

We Love You Whitney

Yesterday you were here today you're gone,
but I know tomorrow that we will see you in Heaven.
You were taken much too soon from us,
our dearest Whitney.
Yet only God knows why and
He knows what's best.
Whitney, you fulfilled your destiny on this earth.
You are a gift that's Heaven Sent.
You were the instrument that
God used in his great orchestra!
Known as The Voice,
you gave no one any choice
but to listen and hear the music for our ears
you sang in the choir,
but little did we know
that we were blessed to be touched by an angel.
Like a butterfly with beautifully hypnotic wings,
you soared above everything with such
elegance, brilliance, and amazing grace.
No other could ever take the place of a queen...
The Queen of Gospel and Pop!
Long live The Queen,
our Star-Spangled Banner
that forever waves in the sky!
We love you, Whitney!

Rainbow in the Sky

Lately, I've been looking for a promise.
I've been searching for a miracle.
I've been hoping for something new and exciting!!
I think I've discovered something all that and
more with a rainbow in the sky!
When things in my life felt like a drought
I had almost every reason to doubt,
God showed me a sign.
He painted the sky and got my attention.
I was fascinated by His design.
He showed me His glory from the heavens above.
His love is pure as a dove.
I enjoy His beautiful rays of sunshine
I am blessed to walk in His marvelous light.
I am amazed at how suddenly a rainbow in the sky
appeared just for me.

Miracles

I need a miracle.
Nothing is too impossible for a miracle.
All we gotta do is put a little hope and prayer in it.
Sometimes, it just shows up and
shows out unexpectedly.
Jesus is the way maker, miracle worker,
promise keeper and light in the darkness.
When we can't see no way,
just know that God sees a way.

His way is giving us the gift
of the embodiment of a miracle.
Nothing about Christ is miracle whipped.
He had to be whipped to death to become
the everlasting miracle that lives in us today!
Miracles are life changing and
they transform atmospheres.
They affect all hemispheres.
No matter where you are on the globe,
a miracle can find its way to you.

Miracles don't have to be chased and
like a comet can make a rare appearance
to light up the sky.
Miracles don't need permission to affect you.
Miracles can shake you up.
Miracles can be groundbreaking.
Miracles are Breakthroughs.
Miracles walk through walls.
Miracles go through the fire!
Miracles are transcendent.
Miracles are of the highest precedent.
Miracles light up the world and they bring us joy.

Miracles can happen to anybody.
They don't happen by accident!
Miracles propel you for greater blessings.
I'm talking about those double-portion blessings.

Miracles are anointed and
they are usually bestowed on us by the heavenly angels.
Miracles have saved many lives.
Miracles have brought new life and new meaning.
Miracles have given someone mercy.
Miracles have protected us from the evil one!
Miracles are praises that go up to our
King of kings and Lord of lords!
Miracles are beyond our wildest dreams.
Just waking up every day to breath in fresh air is a miracle.
Kissing and hugging the ones you love is a miracle.
Coming back home after a long hiatus is a miracle.

Memories can also be considered miracles too.
We remember those we've lost but
we know they are always with us no matter where we go.
Miracles are an anchor. Miracles are the work of the Master!
We are His best creations so therefore
we are His miracles in this world.
We are gifts to one another.
We share versions of our own unique stories or
experiences with each other.
Miracles can be mysterious,
but when they are revealed...
baby, there are nothing like them!

It's a miracle that God is with us.
It's a miracle that God lives insides each of us.
It's a miracle that He loves us.
Miracles show us the goodness of God!
Miracles are always on time and ahead of schedule.

They are never late.
The stars in the sky are miracles we see every night.
The moon and the sun are miracles
we witness each passing day.
The gift of time is a miracle, it's currency.
Living a life of abundance is a miracle.
Be thankful. Count your blessings.
Remember you're a living testimony and
your testimony is a miracle.
People need us more than we think they do.

Miracles can seem to be too much, but don't question it.
You were given this particular miracle for a reason!
Embrace it. Receive it. Enjoy it.
And don't forget to pay it forward.
If we could all work together,
we can achieve anything.
Our miracles will help the next generations for years to come!
Miracles have power!
They have the power to change anything.
Miracles are divine!
Miracles will happen when we have faith
that all things work together for those that love the Lord
and are called according to His purpose!

Dreams Still Come True

Dreams are pictures we see as we are sleeping.
Dreams become a vision when a man or
woman has the courage to believe and carry them out.
Dreams existed long before we were ever created.
Dreams still exist and will exist long after we are gone.
Dreams have no expiration date,
but they do require a sense of urgency.
Dreams can be big, but they can also start off small.
Gotta stand tall and stretch yourself
to grow up to your dreams' potential!

Slips and falls occur, but don't give up.
Your dreams are calling on you to go after them…
achieve what they have to offer.
Sometimes all you have is a dollar and a dream.
There is cream to be had.
Aren't you glad you are so close to finally, having it?
Maybe you already had some of it
because we know that cream always rises to the top!
That's gonna be me real soon, mark my words!
Sacrifice is the down payment to reach your dreams.
The reward for the hard work, struggles, and faith
will all be worth it in the end.
No matter what you heard or thought,
dreams still come true!
I know mine did.

I'm Proud of Me

Sometimes you have to take a
moment to appreciate yourself.
Take a moment to appreciate how far you've come in life,
all that you are, and all that you're becoming!
On behalf of myself, I raise a glass
and give myself a toast.
I'm proud of me in case
you didn't hear me the first time,
I said I'm proud of me!

I have every reason to be after all I've been through.
God saw me through and now I can say
I'm finally experiencing a breakthrough.
It feels really good too.
People tried to break my soul and rob me of pure joy.
The devil is a liar! The truth has set me free
and like Beyoncé, I got a new motivation.
I'm building my own foundation. I'm on a new vibration!
I'm a new creation and I'm enjoying a new Renaissance.
I'm back outside and soaking up the sun
I got new energy and I'm feeling myself it's my party
I'm going to celebrate me today

I got a brand-new walk, talk, and attitude
I wouldn't be where I'm at without
gratitude humility, faith, hope, and love
I had some growing pains and
sometimes I fell flat on my face
there were times I didn't succeed but
it didn't stop me from moving forward
I didn't let the past hold me back or
let the haters keep me from my destiny
I'm proud of what I've been able to accomplish in my life

nothing in this journey came easy
I put something I like to call hard work
blood sweat and tears
what's the cost and all part of the grind!

I walked through the darkness
now it's my time to shine
I'm proud that I have the courage to go for mine
I'm not perfect but I made tremendous progress
stress almost killed me but
I'm still here and I'm the last man standing
I'm built for this life I'm unstoppable
more than capable of doing some real damage
right now I just keeping calm
counting my blessings.

I'm proud of the man I am
I'm different and there is nobody like me
I'm proud of the legacy I'll leave behind someday
I'm proud I've survived everything life is thrown at me this far
I'm proud of how I kept my cool and kept it real
I'm proud of the heart I carry
inside of it there is just so much love to give
I'm proud of what I stand for
I'm proud of what I believe in
I am proud of my transformation
I am proud of me embracing all that I am.
Sighs...I'm just so proud of me!

Waves

As I wave to my crowd, they return the favor and wave back to me!
I love being greeted with kind and warm receptions.
I feel welcome and right at home with all of you.
I am honored to speak with you all today.
I didn't prepare a speech; however, I do have a poem
I would like to recite to all of you. It's called Waves!
I woke up this morning brushing my hair or
what little bit of hair I do have,
in hopes of creating this urban hairstyle called Waves.

Most young black men back in the day
thought it would be fly to rock this special kind of waves.
At first, I thought waves were from the ocean.
But I'll get to that shortly.
Anyway, let me get back to what I was saying, oh yes!
So, it's a process to get these smooth, cool waves!
To earn your waves, one must brush his hair frequently and wear
something on their head called a du-rag!
Some people naturally had waves
some of us had to work a little harder.
Even then I still didn't see any waves on my big ol' head!
In the end, I decided to stick with my fresh fade!
I felt like my soul could glow either way
I felt silky and smooth when I would talk to the ladies.
There was no need for a Jheri curl
that hairstyle got played out a long time ago.
I didn't wanna drip unless it was swimming in a pool or something.
Wait a minute, that's it...
I'm really talking about a change of scenery right.
I'm thinking about the ocean and what is associated with it?

Hmmm...oh yes, WAVES!!

Waves are defined as a long body of water
curling into an arched form and breaking on the shore.
The ocean is never still.
"Waves transmit energy not water,
across the ocean and if not obstructed by anything,
they have the potential to travel across an entire ocean basin.
Waves are most caused by wind.
Wind-driven waves, or surface waves, are created by
the friction between wind and surface water.
As wind blows across the surface of the ocean or a lake,
the continual disturbance creates a wave crest."
(https://oceanservice.noaa.gov/facts/eutrophication.html, 10/05/17).

More potentially hazardous waves can be caused by
severe weather, like a hurricane.
The strong winds and pressure from this type of
severe storm causes storm surge.
Storm surge is the rise in seawater level caused solely by waves.
Other hazardous waves are caused by underwater disturbances that
displace large amounts of water quickly such as earthquakes,
landslides, and volcanic eruptions.
These long waves are called tsunamis!
Waves of this magnitude can cause some massive
damage to infrastructure and can be quite devastating!
The gravitational pull of the sun and moon
on the earth also causes waves.
These waves are tides or, in other words, tidal waves.
Waves move with momentum.
They are a force, and they are powerful enough
to move you to and fro!
Sometimes, surfers like to ride on the waves as a fun activity!
But waves can be dangerous if we aren't careful.
Waves can make a big splash and
in life we need those big splashes from time to time.
Waves go up and down and
make thundering sounds as they come from all directions.

Life is like waves, they can be fun
when conditions are just right,
but can harm you or bring you down suddenly!
Waves should be respected,
a person should never think that they will
overwhelm or overpower the ocean.
Sorry, it's just not happening!
Jesus walked on water.
So, obviously he walked on waves.
God controls the waves, after all He created them.
Waves are like momenta you have in life.
They will carry you only so far until
you have to catch the next one.
Waves hit differently like blessings
that are about to catch you.
Waves are a gorgeous sight
especially when the sun hits them just right.
Sometimes we are awaiting a wave
that we are hoping will eventually come.
I'm waiting on my significant other wave to arrive.
I know my wave will come in the beautiful form of her.
I just have to be patient.
What's your wave?
The waves are coming, just be ready
to receive their messages when they come.
Get ready to cheer on the best that's yet to come.
Let's all do the W-A-V-E!
Enjoy the wave of life while you can because
someday, we will need to wave goodbye.
Life starts off as a ripple and finally grows into a wave.
Then one day we find ourselves in a grave or
our ashes being tossed into the ocean.
Finally, we will be the waves that will become a part of the ocean!
We are all WAVES!!!

40

Rescue

We've all at some points have been in need of rescue.
We're not always going to be on our A game,
so sometimes we get caught slippin'.
Sometimes we just have accidents that are beyond our control.
When you're injured, hurt, or in need of serious medical attention
there is usually help on the way.
Rescue is often imperative and
needs to happen as urgently as possible.
A cry for help is a signal that sounds
the alarm in distress or emergency.

Rescue is assistance to those that are
incapable of helping themselves.
Rescue is a form of hospitality.
It is the difference between life and death.
Some people will refuse to be rescued and
wind up sinking or drowning in their own demise.
Sirens usually go off and you see ambulances rushing
to get to an emergency situation.
Hesitancy and complacency work against the time
needed to rescue a person or people.

Rescue can be a challenge and be a very high risk!
Rescuers put their lives on the line 99.9% of the time.
Sometimes rescue crews are called to assist
someone that may be lost at sea.
Duration of rescues can take anywhere
up to minutes, hours, and days.
Unfortunately, not all rescue attempts are successful!
Rescue helicopters can be dispatched to rain down gallons of water
on uncontrollable fires that break out in certain areas.
Even home/business areas that are flooded out, need rescuing
just like what happened in Hurricane Katrina. ⑨

In relationships, some people feel like they need to
rescue their partner from themselves or
whatever danger they find themselves in.
Some guys feel like they have to be what the streets
call "Captain Save A Hoe."
They feel they have to buy a girl anything to get the drawls.
Another thing that we used to say was
"you can't turn a hoe into a housewife."

Most of these ladies don't want to be rescued anyway but
they will play you if you let them.
Ladies also face the same problem
with all these "fuckbois" running around here.
He could just be a flirt, but it's not cool if he doin' dirt to the lady,
he claims to be his girl.
Dating these days makes you wanna say,
Jesus take the wheel because it so rough these days.
Some people need to be rescued from
heartache, pain, depression, anxiety, and bad decisions.

God is the Great Rescuer, and
He knows just exactly how to save you.
Believe that He will and can rescue you.
He's done it before, and He'll do it again and again and again!
No matter how far you seem to be from God,
He always will meet you where you are.
He will always be with you and there is nothing or no one
that will keep God from getting to you!
Love is what He uses to rescue the world from its own destruction.
Call on God's name anytime and
He will certainly come to your rescue!!

Anchor

Sometimes I feel so bad.
Sometimes I feel so sad.
I wish I had more to give.
I strive to do my best, yet it's not good enough.
The more I live, the harder life gets.
I'm tired of just trying to get by.
I can't even lie, it's not easy to sleep at night.
I've stayed in this fight
enduring an endless battle with trials
and attacks from the enemy.
I've been wounded deeply.
I do everything I can to stand up against the hits and
pressure life too often gives.
God gave me a new day and I'm thankful,
but I need Him in the worst way.
I'm troubled in my spirit and only He knows how
to deliver me from my pain and sorrows.
Please, help me, Lord. I need You!
I can't do this all by myself.
I'm holding on as much as I can, but
I'm at my breaking point.
I need a breakthrough. Breakthrough.
I need You to see me through these passing storms.
I'm having a hard time staying calm and being at peace.
I surrender everything to you this time LORD.
But I gotta ask, why do I have to bear this cup.
The burdens I carry are too heavy.
I need Your yoke for relief.
I need Your touch for blessed reassurance.
My hope and trust are in You LORD.
I know anything is possible with You.
I'm calling out Your name Father.
Where are You?

I'm in distress and You're the only one who can rescue me!
I feel like I'm sinking, please take me into the boat!
Keep afloat with your tender love, grace, and mercy.
Lord, be my anchor ⚓ and
don't let me get tossed to and fro by the wind.
The only thing I want the wind to do is
blow away my worries, doubts, and fears!
I get scared sometimes about
what the future could possibly look like.
I know that You have a plan and purpose for my life.
Plans to bless and prosper me.
You have given me a hope and a future.
I draw near to You because You draw near to me O' God!
I lift up Your name and You lift up my head.
Please keep me lifted in Your righteous right hand.
I know Your promises are on the way.
I take heart knowing that You will provide and
lift my soul always.
You're my anchor!
I am fastened to You always Jesus.
I'm glad You're my anchor!

Paw-sture

I absolutely love dogs.
They come in all different colors, breeds, shapes, and sizes.
Dogs are loyal creatures that serve us as their masters.
In return we must love, respect, and care for them.
We give dogs a residence and they feel welcome in our presence.
At birth they are pups and grow up to be full grown dogs.
They are very cute and can make your heart just melt looking at them.
Their tongues are wagging, and they just love to drool all over you.
They come with fur and enjoy getting petted most of the time!
Their eyes light up with so much joy whenever they see you.

Sometimes dogs are so hyped up,
they just love to run around in open space.
They will roam the streets if they have free reign.
As a pet owner you often must keep your pet on a leash,
so they don't stray too far from your sight.
Dogs can often be territorial at times.
Dogs will bark without hesitation.
Beware because they are not afraid to bite if they must.
Dogs are like children; they need their play time.
I must pause and give them attention when necessary.

I can't help but notice their little or big paws.
Dogs enjoy sniffing me out. They are attracted to my human scent.
Most dogs enjoy being close to me.
They are loyal companions and
are usually excellent company to have around.
I can see why they are called man's best friend!
Dogs carry themselves with such great Paw-sture!
I look forward to becoming a dog owner again someday!
Dogs are special to me and
their Paw-sture will always be something I'll always admire.
We are so blessed to have these amazing creatures among us!

Night Owl

Have you ever gone out at night and
stayed awake almost until the early morning?
Some of us are like freaks that come out only at night.
When the night is young, I know I like to get the party started.
I don't need the weekend to necessarily have a good time,
but it's always something nice to look forward to though!
Especially after working on a Friday
when you're done for the day
everyone scatters like cockroaches
trying to get up out of that job!
Plans are usually made but
sometimes we like to go with the flow.
People like me who enjoy being out at night
are often referred to as "night owls."

We like to take over the night and party it up!
We may go out with friends, have a few drinks,
go to a concert or movie, and
maybe have a date night with someone special.
I do remember having some great nights and
other times some pretty shitty nights too!
But overall, I'd say every night was worth it...
I have no regrets.
I always try to make the best of the night
avoid getting into any trouble or fights.
I've always been the life of the party!
The DJ can get the club rockin'
with some jams that make you wanna dance!
I'm a single guy just trying to live my best life.

I'm a social butterfly and love meeting people.
So, when I meet single ladies,
of course I'm going to talk to them.
I don't see nothing wrong with that at all.

My objective is not to hunt for girls.
I just like to go out and have a great time.
I usually fly solo but it's nice when you meet someone
have a special connection with them.
I could really care less if I meet anyone or not...
if I do, that's great and if I don't that's great too!
No worries!
Sometimes at the end of the night
there is a nightcap situation that could happen, I'm just saying.
When it's time for me to go home,
my final destination is back to my place.
Whatever you like to do at night is your business,
but for me personally my favorite nights are
when I get a goodnight sleep honestly.
I have a date with my pillow and
we are gonna cuddle tonight! Lol.
To my future lady wherever you are,
you can lay on the pillow too or
on my chest to hear my heart beating for you.
And only you!
Night owls eventually have to get some shut eye, don't they?
So, to all my night owls don't forget to get some sleep and
do it all over again tomorrow night!
Hooty whooo!!

Wild Eyes

I have something behind these wild eyes
that hides my wild thoughts.
The hunt begins.
Not to sound creepy, but
I'm like a wild animal
gone out into the wilderness.
My eyes are like a lion, they are about as
savage and wild as they can get!
I got the eye of a tiger.
I don't have any visible stripes but
believe me I've earned them!
By His stripes I've been healed.
Sometimes in the wild you
may be beaten and bruised a bit.
Nature is wild.
My wild eyes can see from a certain distance.
My wild eyes can see through the dark.
I can see you being camouflaged in its deception.
By no means am I stalking you,
we just so happened to cross paths.
Like Scarface, the eyes chico they never lie!
I notice a wild glare in your eyes too.
Your eyes look as if you despise me,
but oh… how they entice me!
Almost like they want to invite me to do a face off.
Your eyes are captivating and
look like they want to take me as your prisoner.
You've rattled my cage of attraction and
it's hard for me to tame this passion of mine.
I must control my eyes because
I don't want to give away my real intentions.
Cuz if I do, I probably would scare you away.
You are not prey, but

I have prayed for you in this lifetime.
My instincts want to instruct me
on the right way to approach you.
Just to be clear, it may seem like I'm hunting you
but I'm just really pursuing you!
My wildest dreams are beyond what I can write or
speak in this moment, but
I gotta tell you that I'm totally WILD for you!
My wild eyes have found what I've been hoping and
searching for all this time!
YOU!

All Natural

In a world where we are surrounded with so much fakeness,
it's refreshing to see something all natural.
Natural selection is the process through which populations
of living organisms adapt and change.
Natural describes something that comes from nature
rather than being man-made. (vocabulary.com)
There are natural environments, natural sciences,
natural resources, natural gas, natural reaction,
natural produce, a natural leader, so on and so forth.

I'm an all-natural man and I'm real as they come.
But what I wonder is where are all the fine,
independent, and natural women at?
I know they are out there, but
I keep seeing these ladies replace their natural
features with plastic surgery.
It's their choice and I understand that,
but that artificial stuff isn't for me.

I prefer a natural woman.
I want to make her feel like a natural woman,
like Aretha Franklin sang about!
I'm all for taking things in their natural course.
Courting and dating are natural for a
relationship to potentially occur!
I'm a natural lover.
I love nature and I naturally love good organic food.
Hmmm. Yum! I have natural God-given ability.

I believe in the supernatural.
Nature has its place, but nature has a soul.
It's human nature to want to be connected with your partner and
be at peace with your natural surroundings.

Being naked is natural,
Adam and Eve once walked the Earth in the nude.
I bare my soul with poetry because
it comes natural to me. I'm just all natural!

Vacation

It always nice to have something to look forward to.
There is always a special occasion to take
a well-deserved break, known as vacation!
Some of us take more frequent vacations than others.
And sometimes, most of us don't stray too far,
so we'll opt for a staycation instead.
There are so many places that I fantasize about going to for vacation.
Every now and then you just need to get away from it all...
the stress, the drama, work, kids, family, church, boredom, etc.
Sometimes you just need to get away from your bubble
or comfort zone too.
I want to go all around the world to tickle my fancy.
Some trips are planned well in advance with reservations.
There is nothing like taking trips randomly and being spontaneous!
Vacations are rewarding adventures.
You can spend them anyway you'd like.
You can get lost in your wildest dreams.
Vacations can be an escape from reality.
Vacations can also reduce stress levels considerably.
You can always find great deals on vacation packages all year round.
I've spent some of my best vacations to places like Hawaii,
Dominican Republic, Las Vegas, and Seattle, just to name a few.
I really would love to go to visit Spain, Japan, Australia, Colombia,
Egypt, South Africa, Puerto Rico, Iceland, New Zealand, and Canada.
I'm pretty much open to going almost anywhere.
I can make any place I go into an adventure.
Today, I'm heading to New York.
I've never been to the Big Apple before.
I'm thrilled to go to an amazing new destination like New York City.
I believe new doors of opportunity and
blessings will come my way while I'm visiting NYC.
The best is yet to come and God has certainly ordered my steps.
I realize now that vacations aren't just

for relaxation, fun, or an escape.
I believe they are also meant to have fellowship with God.
He brought me from a mighty long way.
He is my refuge and hiding place.
I never have to look or travel far to reach Him.
The best vacation I'll ever have is when
I spend eternity with Him in Heaven!

The Soloist

For my selection I will use my favorite instrument
to play the sweet song that's in my heart!
It's nothing complicated,
just something that's dedicated to a precious angel
that God created just for me.
Girl, let me play my symphony and
let's live in the company of our harmony!
Ur the melody that rains from heaven,
you're the water to my soul!
As sure as the sun rises in the east and
sets in the west, you're the best love I've ever known.
I've grown fond of our amazing bond....
you're like the swan that swims on the pond,
so beautiful and graceful you are!
The ripples of the blues disturb the pattern of my heartbeat!
Perhaps the rhythm is irregular,
but you know I love you on the regular!
We are fine-tuned like strings on an acoustic guitar!
The vibration from the drum's percussion beats
with a pounding sensation.
We're the topic of discussion,
everyone has a conversation
about the beautiful music we make!
In the wake of the storm, we form a dynamic duo
of thunder and lightning!
We have a strange relationship;
it's so polarizing but so unique!
Let's clothe ourselves with passion in love's boutique!
We're like new shoes, we both fit together,
and we smell so fresh!
We're the classic of Beethoven,
timeless and legendary!
Like Alicia Keys, I know a woman's worth!

Ur worth more than gold, silver, diamonds, or even pearls...
Ur a treasure that I cherish infinitely!
Your body is my saxophone,
I make you ooze with the infection of jazz!
I'm the bee that's buzzin' to ur honey,
everything about you is oh so sweet!
I'm ur soloist, you'll always be my masterpiece!
Take ur bow!

I Got Your Back

Baby, come over here and let me rub your back.
I know you have been on your feet majority of the day.
I know your back must be hurting.
Don't worry...like a chiropractor
I got your back!

Honey, you're in good hands with me.
I got the right touch, and
I can navigate from your neck all the way down.
I come from out of town, and
I used these frequent flyer miles to come see you.
Seeing you is worth the trip.
However, there is a trip I want to take you on
that will rock your world.
Leave your worries behind and
watch me creep up from behind.
I need you to unwind and let me go to work.
I got your back and I have the dominant position.

I have you in the right hold.
I think you could tap out any minute now.
But you're enjoying how I grab you from the back and
giving it to you so good.
No need for backup
when I'm already the designated backup.
I have control of the entire situation.
I'm not letting up off my grip anytime soon.
So, you better get used to this baby!
No other man is ever gonna run up on you
if I got your back.
That's a fact!

B.E.A.C.H.

There is a place that I desire to often go
that I call my happy place.
It gives me great pleasure,
peace, relaxation, and fun.
I would say it's one of my top favorite destinations.
This place is a national treasure and
it's known to many as the beach.
You can usually expect to be met and
greeted with a warm and radiating sun.

Many people like myself enjoy basking in its glory and
absorbing the sunlight rays on our skin for vitamin D.
The enchanting sand that I walk on
allows me to bury my feet temporarily.
I love to leave footprints on the sand and
leave behind a trail like my past.
When I look beyond the shore,
the waves often catch my eye
and leave me mesmerized.

I can see my future.
I enjoy feeling the cool,
windy breeze blowing against my body.
I don't know how to swim, but
I don't mind getting my feet wet every now and then.
I live for the moment and take it all in stride.
I dreamed of someday living on the beach.
I can see myself owning a high-rise condo
with an amazing view,
overlooking a gorgeous sandy beach.
I would go to the beach day or night and

watch sun rises and sunsets.
I could even envision me and my future wife
laying on the beach together having a romantic rendezvous.
My favorite time to go on the beach is 4th of July.
The fireworks make for a spectacular display
across the dark skies.
If you ever want to visit the beach,
I highly recommend that you do.
It's a place you can have a great outdoor adventure and
have fun in the sun.
It's the best escape anyone can have!

Recovery

I've learned that we must learn to pace ourselves in life.
We all have our own stories and
have all had to come back from something.
You may have come back from an injury,
a setback, a deficit, a legal battle, illness, or rehab.
One of my personal battles
I had to overcome
was my recovery from a recent car accident
that I was involved in.
I was hit by a random car in the parking lot
that wasn't paying any attention.
It left me shook up a little bit,
so I eventually found myself
having to go through physical therapy.
I saw a chiropractor to help me deal with my new normal.
Some days are not good, and
some days are better than others
when dealing with my rating of pain.

Nonetheless I am grateful that it wasn't any worse than it was.
I'm fortunate to be in one piece.
I'm fortunate to still be here.
I'm fortunate to still be doing what I love....
WRITING!

We all are faced with unforeseen circumstances and challenges, but
it's important to choose how we respond to them.
I had to get out of the mindset of why me? Poor me.
I'm learning to change my mind
to change my outlook on things pertaining to my life.
You should too when it comes to your own life.

Things go wrong and nothing is perfect.

Our attitude is key and if affects
how we deal with the recovery process.
Recovery reminds us that we're human.
Recovery shows how resilient we are.
Recovery requires patience.
It requires focus.
It requires discipline.
There is no shame in being in recovery.
We are still in the fight
because we're still alive.

Proud, Tough, Strong, Determined (P.T.S.D.)

They want a muted, toned-down version of me!
I understand there is a time to keep it on the hush,
but I will push back against those
who try to silence or cancel me indefinitely.
I was gifted with a beautiful voice, and
I intend to use it to the best of my ability!
You can't speak down to someone
without expecting them to roar back at you like a lion!
But I have too much to lose,
so I gotta keep my cool.

Sometimes I get tired of playing by the rules,
while other people get to take advantage of their special privileges.
Most of the times they get a pass for the things that they do.
I can't snap, just only when I need to get back to reality.
I have been through quite a few traumatic episodes
that have affected my mental health.
I made the ultimate sacrifice by serving country.
I am a combat veteran that has stepped foot on foreign soil.
I felt strange being in places I wasn't familiar with.
But I feel even stranger as a civilian
trying to function in this ever-changing world.

P.T.S.D. is known as a disorder or mental illness.
In some cases, I struggle with PTSD.
It's not something that just goes away.
Every day I battle with it.
A lot of veterans fight that battle too!
There are no excuses for bad behavior or
poor choices because of P.T.S.D.
Instead of focusing on what has happened to us,
we should focus on what's happening on the inside of us.
PTSD doesn't just mean Post Traumatic Stress Disorder.

It also means the men and women who served
are Proud, Tough, Strong, and Determined!
Together that is what we are, and
we are unified as one!

Hard

Life can be hard sometimes.
It's so hard to deal with the things life can throw at you.
Nothing in this life comes easy.
Hard work is a requirement to pass the lessons
that life's curriculum gives you as a student.
You have much to learn from this life.
There are no guarantees or promises
that you will see tomorrow.

It's hard to accept that most of the time.
It's hard to witness a loved one or friend's expiration date.
It's hard to let go when you want to hold on so tightly.
It's hard being a loser when you fail more times than you win.
It's hard to admit defeat when you just want to be victorious.
It's hard to lose friends that you would like to keep in your life.
It's hard to go through life alone.
It's hard to struggle when things come
much easier for someone else.

It's hard to be wrong when you think you're right.
It's hard to watch things blow up in your face
when you intended for a better outcome.
It's hard to be the button of everyone's jokes.
It's hard to feel like you're helpless and
you desperately want to do something.

It's hard when you get cheated on
by the one you love in a relationship.
It's hard when you can't pay your bills on time.
It's hard when you don't have the strength or
motivation to do anything.
It's hard when you get judged
by people for almost everything.

It's hard to forgive those that hurt, mistreat, or abuse you.
It's hard to give someone a second chance.
It's hard to say goodbye.
It's hard to lose something valuable
that carries sentimental value.
It's hard to lead at times.
It's hard to follow bad leaders.
It's hard to hold your tongue
when you want to say how you really feel.

It's hard to be yourself when people misunderstand you or
don't want to get to know you.
It's hard to waste your time on people or
things that don't add value to your life.
It's hard to say no when you want to say yes.
It's hard to be disrespected or underappreciated.
It's hard to make decisions that aren't easy.
It's hard to sacrifice for someone else.
It's hard to be accountable.
It's hard to be a woman.
It's hard to be a man.

It's hard to put your emotions in check.
It's hard to be human.
It's hard to give labor to a baby.
It's hard to have an abortion.
It's hard to witness someone's self-destruction.
It's hard to stay when you want to leave.
It's hard to wake up when you want to sleep.
It's hard to sleep when you have things
on your mind or things to do. It's hard to be a parent.
It's hard to stay in love.
It's hard to understand what doesn't seem to make sense.
It's hard to fit in.
It's hard to get an education.
It's hard to lose or gain weight.

It's hard to be in the military.
It's hard to be a civilian.
It's hard to love your enemies.
It's hard to be sweet when you're feeling bitter.
It's hard to pay attention when you have a short attention span.
It's hard to choose between what's popular and
what's the best thing to do.
It's hard to be homeless.
It's hard to be jobless.
It's hard to be in prison.

It's hard to pray when you don't feel like it.
It's hard to see someone else get their blessing
when you still are waiting for yours.
It's hard to encourage yourself
when you feel nothing but discouragement.
It's hard to stay focused whenever you are distracted.
It's hard to date nowadays.
It's hard to be in the friend zone.
It's hard to be married when you wanna throw in the towel.
It's hard to look at the man or woman in the mirror sometimes.
It's hard be silent when you should speak.
It's hard to speak when all you want to do is be silent.
It's hard to love and be loved.
It's hard to share your deepest and darkest secrets.
It's hard to be in the dark and
come into the light for everything to be exposed.
It's hard to be broken and becoming whole again.

It's hard to heal.
It's hard to admit when you have a problem.
It's hard to see when you've been blind all this time.
It's hard to break down walls that people put up.
It's hard to be strong when you are weak.
It's hard to admit your weaknesses or flaws.
It's hard seeing someone you love in so much pain.

Certain levels in a video game are hard to master.
Everything has a varying degree of difficulty to it.
You are responsible for figuring out how to master
the obstacles you face.

Choose your hard...nothing will stay hard forever;
you eventually will get it or maybe not.
Don't let HARD stop you
from getting to your objective.
It's OK to ask for HELP.
No one is exempt from getting a little help sometimes
because we don't know everything.
We must learn even if it's the HARD way!
To master the level of Hard,
you too must become HARD!
To be hard you must become
built for the challenge of HARD!
BE HARD!!!

The Heat

Ya'll wanted to shoot at me with your fiery darts...
so now you about to get this heat.
You ignited something fierce inside of me and
I'm about to torch you with this fire ass poem!
You always wanna shine a bad light on somebody but
I am the star of this spotlight!
You mad because ain't none of it on you!
I'm too busy living my best life while
the rest of ya'll mf's is miserable!
Bad vibes are not good for anyone's health.
Ya'll ain't nothing but sick and tired.

You're an infection that I can't have nowhere near me.
You like to spew venom from your deceitful lips.
You're extremely toxic.
I can't have any of your symptoms.
You're beyond a cure.
You're nothing but a chronic illness.
I'm sick of you being around me with all your drama.
Leave that @ home and leave me alone.
If not, you can be quick to get this lava.
The Heat is on!

Thrown Into the Fire

Welcome to the fire!
The heat is on and if you're like me,
you're probably feeling it too!
Temperature is rising and my ass is burning up.
Speaking of burning, you smell that?
I'm getting fried like bacon except without the grease.
There is smoke but I was hoping for the smoke detector to go off!
Someone call the fire department.
I'm just kidding.
But honestly, this is an emergency.
There is a fire and I'm in the middle of it.
Hell, you might be in it too!

Sometimes we may find ourselves thrown into a situation
that we are not adequately prepared or trained for!
Most of us have watched other people put out fires in the past,
but it's a different story when you have to put a few out yourself.
Of course, you're gonna make some mistakes,
but what better way than to learn from them.
When you're thrown into the fire,
those who supervise you are evaluating you
to see if you can handle the pressure.

Being thrown into the fire means that you're being tested!
You can either let the fire burn you or you can put it out.
If the fire is too much for you to handle alone,
don't hesitate to call for assistance!
The objective is to contain the fire and
not let it overwhelm or overtake you!
When you're thrown into the fire,
you need to understand that fire refines us all.
It cleanses us of all impurities!

There is a reason why some fires are called "wildfires."
They can often get out of control sometimes.
Maturity is needed for you to grow.
You can learn so much through any of these fiery moments.
Various fires come with many different challenges.
Sometimes it's all how you look at things as well.
You can get burned or actually be THE FIRE!

When life gives you marshmallows make Smores!
It doesn't always feel good to be in the fire,
but it can be really helpful.
If you want to level up,
you just have to learn to embrace the fire!
Being thrown into the fire
will get you out of your comfort zone!
If it's too hot in the kitchen for you,
I'll take the HEAT! Bring it on!!
Think of yourself as FUEL to the fire!
Let's keep it going.
Just remember that
when you're thrown into the fire!!!

Get to Know Me

Some people don't see me for who I am.
They assume I'm this or that.
Always running off at the mouth like they know so much.
But the truth is, they really don't know me.
Most people like to assume the worst but
won't take the time to get to know a person first.
Don't get me wrong there are a few people
that can see beyond the surface and not judge me.
They admire, respect, and love me for who I am.
Those other folks like to throw red flags
on every good character trait I exhibit.
They are inhibited by their own insecurities and fears.
In my world, hate and discrimination are not tolerated.

Therefore, all the above I've mentioned is prohibited!
I don't give an ounce of space for anyone's disrespect.
If you're with that crap, you can just bounce and
take all that elsewhere.
None of that belongs here.
Yeah, I took it there and
there's nothing you're going to do about it either.
You know you're wrong.
Dead wrong!
I stand on the strength of my faith and
the image of God that I bear.
I wear these blessings like they will never go out with styles.
Why should I care how you feel about me?
You don't want me to be free, so guess what?
I'm gonna continue to exercise my freedom and fight for it!
You don't want me to be me, but guess what?
I'm gonna continue to be me and
become the best version of myself
whether you like it or not!

I have nothing to prove to you.
I'm not perfect but every day I strive to become better.
Some of y'all seem to enjoy being bitter!
Put your anger away and learn to embrace happiness.
If you even know what that looks and feels like.
We all have our moments but
remember that's all what they are.
Don't stay there. Do better. Be better.
Look at yourself before you come steppin' to me.
I know the man in the mirror,
get to know my reflection for your protection.
Stop trying to put a crack in my image.
I'm a whole person that is made
to shine and be beautiful!
Get to know me!

Get in Your Stance

It's been said that styles make fights!
Let's get in our stances.
It's time to dance!
Martial arts are a way to defend yourself or
compete against your opposition.
There are various forms of martial arts.
You have an array of techniques that deliver unique,
fascinating, and sometimes devastating results.
Some of these martial arts include
Muay Thai, Brazilian Jiu-Jitsu, Karate,
Tae Kwon Do, Judo, Kenpo, Roman Greco Wrestling,
Capoeira, Kung Fu, Hapkido, Kick Boxing, etc.

When people are ready to fight or mix it up,
they often like to mix or combine different martial arts!
Martial arts can tell a very compelling story.
It's a language that speaks violence, fierceness, balance,
toughness, discipline, adversity, submission, and triumph!
Whether you're in the octagon, a ring, or in the street,
you must be ready to get into your stance.
Sometimes you don't have to use your
hands or feet to end a conflict.
You can use verbal judo,
meaning you can de-escalate the situation
by having a calm, gentle, and mature demeanor.

Adrenaline kicks in very fast when you are in
a fight or about to engage in a fight.
Although I have been in an actual fist fight,
I know that I can definitely hold my own.
I use a respectful and non-aggressive approach.

The stance that I prefer to use is my stance of peace
and being in a prayer posture.

I believe my faith in God is very strong and
with Him I can't lose!
He goes before me, and the battle isn't mine it's
The LORD's!
We have an enemy that wants to hurt us.
We have an enemy that wants to take us out!
We always must be prepared to do battle with our enemy.
Not all fights are physical, some of them are spiritual.
They are battles you can't see.

This is where your faith comes in.
No weapon formed against you shall prosper!
We will be attacked but are equipped because
The Holy Spirit lives inside of us.
He is our advocate, our comforter, our strength, our shield!
Stand against your foes, but most of all
stand against your greatest enemy, Satan!
God is with us, and we have the victory.
But remember we always should get in our stance!!!

Fight

Never been in a fist fight,
but I'm more than confident
that I could go a few rounds.
Listen I'm not here to pick a fight,
but I might take it there.
Don't tempt me.
I got self-control and
I'm really not about the violence.
But don't get it twisted,
like Drake I can go 0-100 real quick.

Don't think I'm a pushover because
little do you know I push back even harder.
I know how to stand my ground,
I'm not about to let anyone push me around.
I'm a stand-up kind of guy, but
most fights end up on the ground.
The sound of a loud thump should let you know
I can bring you down to earth.
I'm not playing any games.

You started all of this and
now I'm gonna finish it!
Some people underestimated
my kindness for weakness,
but what they didn't know was
how much of a beast I truly am!
They thought they could bully me.
But they couldn't cuz I'm full grown.
I'm a force to be reckoned with!
The way I fight is different than the way you fight.
I want nothing more than to
live in peace and have a piece of mind.

But sometimes people leave me no choice...
I can only be nice so many times.
I can't ignore your crimes any longer, you must pay!

No threats given, but also understand it's also
no fucks given at this point either.
I'm the type to fight with all my heart.
I fight for things that matter like LOVE!!
That's worth fighting for.

I once fought for my country, and it was honorable.
But fighting for my faith is much more fulfilling.
It's an ongoing battle where I'm fighting my demons,
but I already proclaim that I have the victory.
Freedom isn't free.
You must fight for it!
If you don't, we would continue
to be in the institution of slavery.

Some things will try to take you down and
you might get knocked down.
When you're down, remember to will
yourself back onto your feet!
Fight until the bitter end.
Fight your heart out.
Take the fight to your enemy.
Remember that something worth having
is worth fighting for.
So, I say fight on.
Keep fighting.
Stay in the fight!
You have what it takes to win.
Now go out there and win this fight!

Thrown Under the Bus

I grew up on a street called Buss
and eventually found myself riding on many more buses
throughout my lifetime.
Buses are designed for transportation
by carrying passengers to reach desired destinations.
Buses drop you off and pick you up on certain routes they take.
Nothing wrong with taking the bus,
might take a while to wait on them though.
Now, I know most of us have heard the expression,
"I got thrown under the bus."
Or, he or she threw me under the bus!

What that means is someone told on you for something
you might have done that you weren't supposed to do.
Or, possibly called you out
in front of everyone just to single you out!
I've been on that ship a few times,
it didn't feel good at all.
I was pissed because I was thinking to myself
you got nothing better to do than to tell on me.
Why couldn't they just talk to me?

I'll admit as I've matured, I realized
they were just lessons and
I had to remember those things would soon pass.
It's still annoying as fuck though.
It's never cooled to be a snitch or a Karen.
I'm sure I've thrown a few people under the bus in the past
as I'm sure we all have done at some point in our lives.
I've learned that if you have a problem with the way
someone is saying or doing something,
go have a conversation with them first.
If you don't feel comfortable,

bring in a neutral party to address the issue.
Problem solved.
So, don't be the person
throwing someone under the bus anymore!

Boundaries

You can be so loving and giving that you often forget
to set your own limits and limitations.
I do believe we call them boundaries, don't we?
Personal boundaries or personal space is needed
so that we don't feel taken advantage of
or feel violated whatsoever.
We draw our invisible lines in the sand.
Sometimes we may feel the need to put up walls
or fence to keep out intruders.
Some of us tend to evade opposition
or retreat into our comfort zones.

It's time we all take a stand and
resist the opposition that tries to come into our territories.
We don't own the land, but we do have the right to our space!
It's ok to give people fair warning
and if they violate your boundaries then you can cut them off
or deny them access to your personal space.
We as people need to learn to respect one another's boundaries.
I know sometimes we may not intend to cause harm but
when you are alerted by someone that tells you no
or its not ok, then that's what they mean.
Point blank!

It's about being aware and respectful of individuals wishes
that we should honor.
I didn't always have boundaries and
now I've set some boundaries up to protect myself.
We should all protect ourselves.
Safety is paramount!
On properties you may see signs that say
Keep Out, Private Property, Warning, or Beware.
These are signs to tell you that your presence

is not welcomed on their property.
They have a right to not have anyone
just trespass on their property.

I know even in relationships you need to have boundaries.
You must be careful and be sensitive to your partner and vice versa.
Boundaries are measures taken so that no one
gets hurt, confused, or lost.
I'm glad I understand what it means to have boundaries
because I know how to not only protect myself
but also protect others too.
Boundaries are necessary and
I'm all for them.
Make sure you set up your boundaries
because it's for your own good!

The Way I Spit

Ya'll so quiet...
let me start a riot
up in here one time!
My pen moves steady in silence,
but its deadly.
I'm ready to flip the script.
My words march out of my brain
and deliver on site.
I come riding in on my lyrical chariot.
I'm straight from the Underground like Harriet.

I'm not afraid to bust...
I will if I must…
to get my point across.
I speak my mind and
let it slice your craniums like a Samurai.
Cold blooded assassin on the mic.
I'm from the 707...yeah,
I got that Cali connection for life.
I stay cuttin' up like a knife.
I'm known to spill my guts unless
you wanna trade places with me.
It takes a real one to stand up for himself
and fall on his own sword if he must.
I have my wounds,
but in time they will heal.
Trust...
I am a warrior that just so happens to be a poet.
You can quote this for your own reference...
everything I ever spit,
I wrote it!

Coward

You're a coward!
You stooped so low to do something so low.
You're nothing but a spineless coward!!
You put your hands on someone I love dearly.
You're so lucky I didn't put that hurt on you!
I wanted to rip you apart!
It's a miracle you're still even walking around breathing.
I don't condone violence except
when it comes to hurting those I love.

I believe cowards should pay the ultimate consequences!
Thankfully, I have Jesus in my heart.
I believe God has changed me for the better.
Now all I wanna do is pray for you.
In my eyes you're still a coward
but I know God will deal with you in His own way.
Be thankful I'm not like you,
I could have done a lot worse to you.
It's not a threat, this is a promise!
Vengeance is mine saith the Lord,
so I honor His word and believe that He will repay.
He is merciful but He is also a judge.

You talked all that smack but couldn't say none of it to my face!
I'm bold enough to say what I need to say in your face.
That's the kind of man I am,
but my words are more effective in prayer.
Men are not supposed to be cowards.
It's unacceptable and can't be tolerated!
Bullying is for cowards and the world had no room for them.
I have never been a fan of cowards; they have no honor.
They don't deserve any respect!
You get no flowers for being a coward.

Cowards should not get any celebration.
Cowards are a disgrace!
But if God can show amazing grace to a coward,
then I'll move forward and forgive a coward.
Greater is He that is in me than he that is in the world.
In the land of the free and home of the brave and abroad,
cowards always will exist unfortunately.
So, cowards beware,
stay the hell out of my way!!

Courage

I am a man of courage.
I'm armed with my own arsenal of skills to go along with it.
A man with courage is quite dangerous...
that means he can't be fucked with!
Excuse me, if I let certain cuss words fly out...
they come straight outta the mouth of a true badass!
I been through a lot of shit in my life.
Thank God,
I made it out of boot camp during my basic military training.

The real test began when I got out
and had to be on my own!
I was full grown, and I've stood on core values
to get me through whatever life threw at me!
I never been the type to ever back down from a challenge.
In fact, I welcome the chance to meet them head on.
I relish every opportunity I get to prove myself against all odds!
Like a deck of cards stacked against me,
I made the best out of my hand to play with.
I went to war in foreign lands, and
I battled each day of adversity with grit and determination.
A man with courage has nothing to lose.
A man of courage will stare down his opponent
with fierce intimidation even when he is afraid.
A man of courage knows he can end a fight before it even begins.
I'm a man of courage who stands tall.

I am a tower of power...
my courage is a terror because
I'm relentless and will pursue greatness
no matter what the cost!
Even when a man of courage falls, he gets back up
like the warrior that he is and continues his fight.

A man of courage will speak his mind and
not be a "yes" man all the time.
A man of courage isn't afraid to get his hands dirty and
get in the ring with the best of them.
A man of courage is an inspiration and admired by many!
I have the courage of a lion.
I learned to hunt in the wild and please believe

I'm a King of The Jungle.
I roar with pride knowing
that I am a man of courage.
And I roar for all those men
who are courageous just like me!
Courage is the highest badge of honor
for any man to receive.
Remember the man who left his mark
and respect a man of courage!

I Done Been to War

I done been to war
I got plenty scars to prove it!
I've never been to hell
but I sure went through it!
I trained in the heat.
Had to beat feet walking through the sand.
I never been a fan of being a casualty.
I can't let nobody bomb on me
unless I bomb first!

I'm a walking target but I
can explode any given moment.
My pain is like shrapnel.
Its cuts real deep!
My wounds bleed for some attention,
not to mention for some love too!
I used to get pissed, but seeing a therapist
makes the healing so much better.
I'll always be a warrior.
I stay doing numbers.
Droppin' hot bars in these nice cars.
I'm back to what I do best.

I'm making my old lady see a few stars,
afterwards she might even get put to sleep.
I've been a Savage way before Meghan ever was...
I stay strapped and equipped if ya know what I mean.
My arsenal is sick with it!
I was in Baghdad when bombs were over it like Outkast!
I outlasted my foes.
Not everyone can wear these shoes I've been in.
I done been to war
and I made it all the way there and back!

Best Friends Forever

I woke up in the morning
craving some hot caramel cappuccino...
or maybe someone else!!

As I walk through the door of the coffee shop.
My eyes met the gaze of a beautiful stranger.

I felt like I walked into a casino and
instantly hit the jackpot!
Your beauty stunned me momentarily
like a taser gun.

I couldn't move for a few seconds,
your gaze almost turned me
into stone like Medusa.

But I'm the Man of Steel
and I wasn't afraid to fly over to you!
Say hello to your Superman.

****

(*Felicia*)
You walked in and my heart stopped...
As your gaze met mine,
the beating of my heart drowned out the noise
of the crowed coffee shop...

And in an instant my wild heart wondered...
Is it possible....
For my wild soul to ache for a stranger?...
For you and this undeniable connection...

All the possibilities came rushing in...

Could you love me in the blinding heat of a birthing star,
when I shower warmth on distant moons?

Could you love me in the hole of the cosmic Black,
where no one can reach me?
Not even you?

Can you love me then too,
without any benefit to you?
Can you love me when I am rough and
wild as I drag my abandoned dreams
through the dirt for days,
to the rhythm of my own ancient drum?

Will you love me if my layers hide all the scars and
wars in my heart, from the images and
feeling and battles I cannot explain?

Will you love me when I lack courage,
when I am defeated,
when I run from you and blame you and
when I won't let you patch my wounds?

Will you trust me when I smell
of the moons sweetgrass and sage,
and when I stink of no rest,
blood, war, whiskey and sweat?

When I drink from the cup of Spirit
and play in astral light,
will you sensually bring me back to my body gently
and anchor me to back Home?

What happens when my words don't work,
my hands are broken and
when I can speak only with my eyes?

Can you love me enough to let me go,
and dance freely on your own
without asking me where I'll be?
I am no machine and
I am no pet laying obediently at your feet.
I am the lone wolf that knows herself
and fetches bones of truth."

Yes, a wild woman.
Not a girlfriend.
Not built for animal wifery.
I am a force. Generative POWER.
A cause for an effect.
I am a structure and have a mission.

I wonder...
Are you afraid to let me inside you?
Not just my flesh, but my soul.
Can I bring you deeper,
are you willing to not run
from your own pain dear King?
The wild woman is neither burglar or vandal.
I will not take anything from you.
I am true to myself and will honor you.
I will not trample on your barely sprouting seeds or
take your fears as trophies.

I am the sun on flooded fields and
the fire for tangled webs,
as I witness with all my heart and
no separation of thought…
And just like,
I am brought back,
delirious from all we could be…

All is Forgiven

Are they pulling for me or pulling away from me?
Every time you see me pull up...you straight skurrrttt!!!
It seems like my presence spooks you like I'm a boogeyman!
You just two steps or do the running man every time I see ya.
I'm gonna keep it real thorough wit ya
cuz I'm a real thorough bred!
You turned your whole back on me.
You distanced yourself from me.
I hope I didn't burn any bridges but
at least let me have a ladder to reach you!

I feel like you left me to burn. You forgot about me.
Why did our friendship disintegrate?
Is this what we gotta do...let it burn like Usher?
It's hard to concentrate on things when everything just went left.
When you left...you left.
I did my thing too! There was no contact.
If there were any hang-ups, it would be the one I got from you.
So, I guess I am left with wondering
why our friendship had to end.

I won't pretend that I was perfect cuz I know I wasn't.
Neither were you. But at least I can say I was wrong.
What about you? Loyalty is a rare breed.
It's something we all need.
My heart bleeds for a reconciliation.
It's still bleeding love for you even though I still hurt.
It still bleeds even when we both did dirt.

My pen and paper are my anesthesia.
I'm human and I feel pain just like everyone else,
but sometimes I become numb.
My feelings grow cold at times.

Deep in my soul I'm still here for you.
Don't know if you feel the way about me...
but let's pull our heads out of our asses and figure this shit out.
Look, I'm sorry!!! Forgive me.
If you're sorry, be sorry...
but let's move past this.

If you're not then don't even worry about it...
I'm not even mad cha!
God heals the broken and makes everything all whole.
I'm convinced we will make amends sooner or later.
So, from where I sit, I'll always keep rooting for you,
but in the meantime I gotta keep pushing forward.
It wasn't always love, but this time
that's exactly what this is...LOVE!!!
All is Forgiven...

Thirsty Man

You're on a mission to find a wishing well.
You find yourself searching for any drop you can get
in the middle of the Sahara Desert.
It's hot as hell and you start to get cotton mouth.
You've traveled so many miles, near and far but
there ain't no supply of drip anywhere in sight.

Then off into the distance
you see a beautiful woman moving in your direction.
You think to yourself that maybe she's your only chance.
So, you just hoping and wishing
that you could just get a sip.
And you get the courage to shoot your shot.
Your lips are so dry that you lick them like LL Cool J.
You open your mouth but
the only thing you seem to do is stutter.
Just a bunch of gibberish
like you forgot what you wanted to say.
She looks at you a bit puzzled,
but she seems to want to invite you
for some kind of pleasant conversation.

You got her attention, so say what you need to say.
Don't blow it dummy!
You somehow find the courage to ask her
where you can find water.
She tells you something you didn't quite expect.
She tells you that she has water on her
and offers you a drink.
Then you say, are you sure?
She smiles and winks, replying yes, I'm sure.
I excitedly told her thank you
and drank water from her canteen.

It was a miracle to find water
from a perfect stranger in a foreign land.

She says, you were really thirsty.
I said, of course but I'm thirstier for you.
The beautiful young woman giggles and blushes.
You offer something for her trouble.
She is surprised that she gets something from you in return.
It's a small token of appreciation.
You then tell her what you want in return.
She says sure anything.
You then tell her to give you every last drop of her.
After all I am a thirsty man!

Tap

As I'm asleep, I feel a tap on my shoulder.
Am I dreaming or did I get tapped for real?
I see a beautiful woman standing over me
and she smiles at me beaming with joy!
She appears to be an angel.
I don't see any wings on her.
But I hope she stays awhile and doesn't fly away.
I'd like her to keep me company just for a little bit.
I can't take my eyes off of her.
She just gazes at me intently, but no words are spoken.
I begin to wonder if she is a messenger
trying to tell me something.
I'm all ears, but I know I'll soon be in tears
because I know she's not really real,
she probably just an illusion.
Pardon my confusion,
my vision is blurred when I don't get enough sleep.
Maybe it was God tapping me to get my attention.
I hop out of my bed and begin tapping my feet.
Life is like a tap-dancing session;
you have to keep those happy feet moving
to create the rhythm you want.

However, don't let your slip be your fall.
Like a soldier, you gotta get up and stand tall.
Head up, shoulders back!
Get in formation...
if you're taller than the person in front of you,
tap them on the shoulder and move forward.
Remember to hydrate,
don't worry about if you're drinking from tap water.
It ain't gonna hurt ya.
If you don't like it...you can hydrate and press on!

Can somebody tell me where my M-9 pistol is?
I'm deadly accurate when it comes to me hitting my target.
I always knew how to double tap.
My opposition gets caught with their pants down.
I always knew I had what it took,
I just had to "tap" into my potential or zone.
My lady know I can tap into her stuff.
I transform into a supersayan,
but she ain't ready for these dragon balls!

All jokes aside, in order to tap into something,
you first must have access!
I want and need access to whatever space is available to me.
I will then claim it as my real estate.
Tap into God's Word to get spiritually fed and filled.
Tap into the source. Tap into your faith.
Tap into The Holy Spirit.
Tap your friend or loved one on the shoulder
to greet them or say goodbye.
Or tap them to make sure they are alive;
they just might be hanging on for dear life.
Don't forget about the "tap,"
it might be the last one you'll ever do for them.
With that being said,
to all my fallen soldiers let's remember them
with the playing of T.A.P.S.
One final tap!

My Voice is my Weapon

My voice is my weapon...it comes armed and dangerous!
There is power and velocity behind the words that I speak.
My voice is like the sound of a platoon
and I'm always ready to give the order.
My words not only drop the mic,
but they also drop like bombs in the surrounding area.
The words we speak often can be considered
weapons of mass destruction.
There are so many casualties and injured persons in a war of words.

Words can inflict severe damage,
but they can also bring medicine of healing.
My words have been harsh and brutal at times,
but they have also been encouraging, inspiring,
and loving at other times too!
We have spoken blessings and cursing out of the same mouth.
I would prefer my words to be seasoned with salt
and flow out like milk and honey.

I can take ownership of what I say
and be more careful with my voice and tone.
Our words can turn someone's sadness into gladness.
Even someone else's kind and comforting words
can do the same for us in our moments of grief and despair.
Our words can be heard from
the North, the South, the East, and the West!
Words provide commentary like the morning and evening news.
Sometimes we just have to stay tuned in
for what the next narrative will be.
The voice we have can spew out flames
that comes from the pits of hell.
Voices can be like sirens,
crying out for help in desperate emergency.

There is a sense of urgency in my voice
and many others for God to hear us.
For anyone to help us in our time of need.
My voice is a force to be reckoned with.
My voice changed in puberty
and transformed in the sound of a mature man!
My voice is huskier, deeper, and sexier than ever.
Sometimes the ladies hang onto every word that I speak.
But with that same voice, I've also messed up many relationships.
The old saying goes, loose lips sink ships!
These same lips would love to make amends
by kissing all my mistakes goodbye.
My voice is my instrument.
Your voice your instrument.
No one knows it better than you do.
You can make your voice the sound of a pleasant whisper
or a loud and obnoxious annoying sound.

Our voices need to be listened to at just the right volume.
But at other times, it just needs to be
turned down or just be silent.
Your voice allows you the freedom to speak your truth...
so go ahead and speak your truth!
Remember that we all are remembered
by the words we spoke after we depart this earth.
You can choose to forget what was said by forgiving it
and throwing it into the sea of forgetfulness.
Just try not to hear the echo ever again.

In my closet
Is where I speak to HIM, I lift my voice to GOD
When things seem grim
GOD hears my voice, HE hears my cries
He gives me wisdom in the place of my whys
(Katrina Taylor's "ChocolateDaPoet" part)

My voice is my weapon and I'm licensed to carry
I can shoot it off when things seem scary
Your words will lead you to success or defeat
The road to obedience is where faith and works meet
It's up to you to make the choice to
Fight with the armor of GOD
Learn to use your voice
Release your faith in words
What's your love language like
Into your situation
Speak the words of life

I use my voice as my weapon
Commanding the mountain to move
I have a different mindset
Dancing to a brand-new groove
Into my purpose I'm steppin'
Don't be led by deception
Put your faith in the LORD
Use your voice as your weapon

Don't Panic

Don't panic, I got this!
You got nothing to worry about cuz
your man knows how to take care of this situation.
I'll show you how I get shit done!
I'm not afraid to take control and risk it all.
I'm ready.

I'm your protection and you can be rest assured that
I'm gonna see us through.
You're probably thinking how exactly am I gonna do that?
Well, my answer is simple.
By trusting God because He is all divine, powerful, faithful,
all knowing, all telling, all mighty, all truth, and all loving!
I submit to His authority because
I know God is the one who is in complete control of everything!

Nothing surprises God.
God fears nothing.
God worries about nothing.
God has no doubts.
God is undefeated!
In God in whom we trust, whom shall we fear?
Don't panic baby,
God has equipped me to handle what I need to handle.
But God is the answer.
He is The Way, The Life, and The Truth.
He is the True Vine.
God will surely take good care of us.
He promised is that He would and I believe Him.
You should too!

Tell Me Girl

Tell me one thing sweetheart
do you want to be with me?
I can't read your thoughts
so tell me what's on your mind

I want to know
whatever there is to know about you girl
you're like a mystery
so much for me to wonder and discover
let me be the one to put a smile on your face
because I really want to see myself and your smile
tell me true and tell me so
because the truth really does count

So baby what's it going to be
I'll stay if you want me to stay
and I'll go if you want me to go
tell me how and
I'll find a way back to your heart
babe I promise you.

Unsung Hero

The Unsung Hero...
a person that is almost never in the spotlight
and whose heroism or achievements are unacknowledged.
Sometimes the unsung hero is unknown or very little known.
Little to no respect is put on the unsung hero's name.

In fact, he is nameless,
the credit never seems to go to the unsung hero!
However, when people are looking for someone to blame
that man's name is quick to be brought up!
Unsung heroes deserve so much more.
They should be adored, not ignored!

To all the hustlers, parents, single mothers,
teachers, student doctors, and front-line soldiers
if no one else sees you, I do.
Keep doing what you do.
One day you'll rise to the top
and get the recognition you truly deserved.
I stand with you because I too,
am an unsung hero!

Makin' Moves

Lately, I've been making moves.
Sometimes I don't know whether I'm coming or going.
So much work has to be done, it's a constant grind.
In order to grow, you have to suffer for it!
I'm trying to be in a better position in life,
but I have to move a certain way and take some risks.
One false move can take you down.
Each move you make needs to be made
with confidence and boldness.
Each move needs to be calculated and visualized.
Sometimes we make the wrong moves
and we can beat ourselves up for it.
You think I should have known better,
but listen don't beat yourself up about it.

Life is trial and error.
Most things we don't have control over
except our mind, mouth, and reactions.
Money and time play a big essential part
for someone making moves!
Money and time control leverage and power.
Some moves are about making the right adjustments.
Money is the reward for solving a problem.
The chase for money burns most people out
from the relentless pursuit of it.
Some people wish they had extra time.
Time is always a factor when it comes to decision making.
Moves can be stalled if there is a hold-up in time or money.

Moves can be held up in procrastination
or for a lack of discipline.
No one is going to take that step for you.
You have to take steps to get where you want to be!

Some of the significant moves I made in my life
is when I joined the military, moved to Florida,
buying a house and writing books!

Moves require some preparation, skill, faith, and discipline.
Moves navigate you to move in a certain direction.
Fear handicaps you from ever making a move.
I'm glad I made moves because
I would still be stagnating in a place
I should not have been in period.

Making moves especially great ones
make you wanna flex!
You start feeling accomplished
and proud of what you did!
That's how I do it.
And I'll continue to make moves
and be successful in reaching my goals!
You do the same.
You got this!

Last Dance

I look at you from a distance like as a spectator
who admires what he sees.
I see a chance and I do hope
we can make a connection.
Honestly, I fear you won't be interested in me
but I'm still going to try and go for it.

What do I have to lose?
I'm brave and I'm courageous.
But you seem dangerous,
but that's a risk I'm willing to take.

I speak to you waiting
to hear your sweet voice.
I'm hoping that we'll be on
the same verbal frequency.
Maybe we have some good vibes.
Maybe we won't.
But it's worth a shot.

This is a delicate dance.
As a man I have to take the lead,
it's up to her to follow.
I took the steps to meet her,
now she has to be convinced
that I can sweep her off her feet.

I don't do fairy tales,
but I think I found my Cinderella.
If she rejects me,
I'll still have my dignity and
I'll be covered with an umbrella of confidence.

I know how to dance in the rain.
I'm no Mary Poppins,
but I know I can get any party poppin!
If she says yes, we can pop champagne and toast it up!
I know I'm silly, but you got to know
how to have a good sense of humor sometimes.

I'm a great dancer plus romancer.
I'm the type of fella
that's been through many dances in life.
There isn't a dance that I can't learn.
Like Whitney,
I've been wanting to dance with somebody.

Not just anybody though.
I need to dance with somebody
who might love me
the way I might love them in return.

I don't mean to step on any toes,
actually I do mean to because
I'm not tripping over any of my mistakes.
I'll keep dancing even if the mood or song changes.

The rhythm of my heart is pounding,
and she has me feeling a certain type of way.
I'm not gonna sell her on anything
or try to be something I'm not.

I can only be ME.
If that's not enough for her,
then it's her loss not mine.
Maybe she just might have her eyes open.
Timing is everything right?

I'm not sure how many dances I have left.
But like Donna Summer,
I would hope this would be my
LAST DANCE.
My last chance for love!
So, what do you say,
will you dance with me?

Move On

I can't walk on eggshells. I can only be me!
I don't know any other way to be except be me!
I'm sorry if you can't accept that, it's just the way it is!
I try my best to take your feelings
and best interests into account,
but I can't just keep dancing to your rhythm
if you can't dance with me.
If only you just knew my heart.
I really mean no harm. I really don't.
That's not my character and it's not part of my DNA.
My intentions were to make you smile
and hoping that we could be friends...I can't lie though,
I would love to be more than a friend if you'll allow it.
So, if nothing else,
I'd rather have you as a friend than not have you at all.

Right now, I'm heartbroken.
As a man, I don't often like to admit such a thing,
but I do have feelings.
My eyes could cry rivers at any second,
so I'm trying to keep myself together.
I really care about you, but the last thing I would ever do
is hurt you or make you feel uncomfortable.
I still think the world of you and
I hope you would think that way of me too.
I heard what you said, and I felt that.
It felt like an earthquake, and it shook me to my core.
There are faults that I carry...
but the love I have inside of me is no disaster.

Sometimes the things I have said
and done have been complete disasters...
but like after any natural disaster there is recovery.

It is my hope and prayer that we can recover from this!
If not, then I understand.
I'm not a bad person and neither are you.
We just had a misunderstanding.
Forgive me. I only want the best for you.
If separation is best, then I'll give you the space you need.
I'll miss you, but I have to move on!
It's nothing personal.
God bless you always!

Elevate

It's time to Elevate.
What do you mean by elevate?
I'm glad you asked.
It means to lift up or make it higher.
It also means to raise in rank or status.
It is to improve morally, intellectually, or culturally.

Like Drake, the only obligation is to tell it straight.
So that's what I'm here to do.
Elevating is a better way to be happier and
more successful in life.
More comes with the territory and
to whom much is given much is required.
The process can often come slowly,
but one move from God can come swiftly.

I never knew patience,
so me and her had to learn how
to get better acquainted.
I thought mistakes would taint
what I was over here trying to build.
But that's far from the truth.
Nothing ever comes easy
and nothing ever grows from stagnant places.
Every level you ascend or aspire to be on
requires a different version of yourself.
I challenge myself to be better more and more each day.
The goal isn't perfection, I just want to make progress
and make my ascent onto the top of the mountain.
Sometimes we have a little too much on our plates.
Every now and then we have to learn how to delegate.
Every now and then elevation requires separation.
Meditate on wisdom and gratitude.

Don't hesitate to take a step forward.
Even if you fall, you can still get back up and try again.
Run your race at your own pace,
don't worry about who's ahead or behind you right now.
You'll get to your destination
at the time you are designated to be there.
Marinate on that for a moment!

I'm educating you on pure facts!!
Don't hesitate to apply the knowledge.
Elevation will accelerate you into the future.
Dreams will eventually catapult you
into higher rewards and blessings.
You'll be prosperous and generate
multiple streams of income.
If it doesn't make dollars,
then it doesn't make cents.
Stay motivated and dedicated,
you can have whatever it is you desire!

Increase will come with an abundant mindset.
Leave your frustrations, doubts, worries,
and fears at the door.
Celebrate every victory
even the little ones along your journey.
People will always speculate
or try to discredit your success.
Just keep doing you and shake off all the hate.
Don't take the bait!

It's not how you start but how you elevate
to get to the finish line is what truly matters!
I'm elevating myself to go above and beyond.
I will have what I deserve.
My friends, elevate and the same will happen to you,
I promise you!

Orbit

Many moons ago I told the stars about you.
Hoping, wishing, and praying for someone like you.
Days turn into nights and months turn into years.
I've waited so long for you to catch just a glimpse of me.
I knew as long I was patient enough,
somehow you would find your way into my orbit.

The stars somehow aligned just right.
Now here we are.
I came this far just to meet the woman
of my dreams face to face.
All that's between us is space and opportunity.
I feel an attraction to you that's as strong as gravity.
I would think the feeling is mutual
because otherwise you wouldn't be
in my presence this very moment in time.

My hands want to travel and land themselves
around that fine waist and crescent-shaped bottom.
I navigate different areas and
I notice you have no craters.
Your surface is so smooth and
I just love gliding my way all over your anatomy.
I want to live in your shadow
so that we can become an eclipse.

We cover and complement each other so well.
If your pants were a glove, I'd fit right in.
Ohhhhh...that's gonna be the sound
of how it's going down.
Like Omarion, let me hear you say ohhhhhh!
Baby, I'm invading your planet and I'm taking over.

Please feel free to swallow me up inside
your galaxy and welcome me home.
I'm your welcomed guest.
Hopefully you found my pleasure encapsulating!
I enjoyed watching you explode with passion.
I'm so glad you found your way into my orbit!
Please stay for a while,
because you'll never want to leave this orbit again!

Sabotage

I know there's a saying out there about
"Don't play the victim."
We don't want to operate from a weak position obviously.
However, there are times that you can legitimately
be a victim when certain circumstances are
beyond your control or comprehension.
There is a tension in the air that you can cut Like a Knife.
There is an elephant in the room
that I'm going to talk about called sabotage.

Yo, hear me out on this one.
The definition of sabotage is a deliberate action
aimed at weakening an enemy through
subversion, obstruction disruption and/or destruction.
Or to deliberately destroy or damage something
to prevent it from being successful in our lives
in some way shape or form,
have been sabotaged by people
or entities that don't have our best interests at heart.

Sabotage is a subtle but very deadly weapon
that can harm an individual's character or reputation.
Sabotage is a stumbling block to use
as an obstacle against someone to prevent them
from reaching a goal or an objective.
Sabotage is deeply rooted in jealousy, fear, and insecurity.
Friendships, relationships, careers, marriages,
businesses, and health can all be affected by sabotage.
It's a disease that spreads like a wildfire.
Sabotage devastates and infiltrates into your soul.
Sabotage leaves a wound that needs healing.
It can make you angry, bitter, depressed,
or even give you anxiety.

Sabotage can be disguised in so many things.
It can be a wolf in sheep's clothing.
Sabotage can be directly linked to betrayal, fraud, and abuse.
Sometimes, I see people with their entourages
that they seemed so close with,
but little do they know that sabotage can strike without warning.

The enemy seeks and destroys.
We must be on guard against the adversary's barrage.
Sabotage likes to lurk in the dark.
It can be camouflaged in deception
and be very reckless with its intentions.
Discernment, The Word of God, and prayer
are weapons you can use to fight against sabotage.
Sabotage has no honor and we must not pay any homage to it.
Sabotage is like a sniper that has victims in his crosshairs.

Get behind cover, don't let sabotage cripple or take you out!
Understand the assignment and
engage the enemy we know as sabotage.
We have come of age.
Alignment, Growth, and Evolution
is our execution for excellence in Warfare of sabotage.

Lies...All Lies

As I sit back and I watch you begin to speak
with those pretty lips of yours,
I already know you are gonna tell me something
that I may want to hear.
It's like sweet music to my ears...
nothing but LIES...ALL LIES!!!

I sit back listening to a serenade of lies
rolling off your tongue.
You are convinced you are telling the truth.
But baby, you're so ruthless with it.
You are so cold with it.
I don't even know what to do with it.
You're so delusional, it's fucking insane!
You're so conceited about your deceit...
my brain can't even believe or comprehend it!

The shit you say makes no damn sense;
I don't think you even believe it!
You're a good actress.
You laid up in my mattress every night
telling me how good it was to ya!
Turns out you were laying in between
the sheets with someone else.
I wrestle with the thought of you
ever loving me or was I just playin the fool?
I fell in love with an undercover liar.

My desire was activated, now its long gone
and I've become aggravated!
Everything about you was counterfeit.
Nothing about your character
screams out authenticity to me.

Lies are a habit that eventually becomes your character!
Lies can seem beautiful on the surface but once they become
discovered or unraveled, they are ugly as can be!
I can't even stand the sight of you.
I just feel sick to my stomach, and I literally could vomit.
But since we are getting everything out in the open,
I cheated too!
I cheated myself for being with someone like you.
So, now I'm moving on to what lies ahead.
You're dismissed and take your lousy lies with you!
Lies...ALL LIES!!!

Loyalty

Loyalty what does that word mean to you?
Loyalty means different things to many people.
For me Loyalty means having a close bond
or partnership with someone that is unbreakable.
Loyalty is stability and you have built up trust
and confidence over a period of time.
Loyalty offers a sense of devotion
and dedication to success.

Loyalty is faithful, trustworthy, and long-suffering.
Loyalty is a leadership trait that should be practiced
and taught to everyone.
Loyalty gets tested at times.
Even at every turn loyalty can be questioned.
Loyalty is a form of respect, admiration, and allegiance!
A lot of things are at stake when it comes to loyalty.
Loyalty comes with strong ties.

Trust is the key to loyalty.
Opportunities for love, intimacy, friendships,
communication, job security, leadership roles,
and more can open up doors due to loyalty.
Loyalty comes with rewards and benefits.
I'm a man of loyalty and I'm loyal to those who are loyal to me.
I am loyal to serving God, my family,
my friends, and to my community.
Loyalty is my way of saying thank you and I will serve you.
But I'm no fool either. Loyalty comes at the expense of betrayal.
Be careful of where or who your loyalty lies.

Allegations

All the chatter doesn't matter.
People getting fatter off these lies you tell.
Eating up everything that you giving them
from your terrible menu of deception.
You cook up nasty allegations and
you like stirring up a hot mess!
Look at you over here being all sloppy.
They say if you can't take the heat
then get out the kitchen.

Clearly, you're sweating over nothing.
I just can't take your onion breath,
so your opinion of me makes no difference.
I'm larger than life.
You wanna give me strife, but I'm the knife
because I'm way sharper than you'll ever be!
You threw me under the bus for no reason,
so what the hell did you expect from me?

I had no choice but to defend myself.
You tried to bury me, but I'm resurrected now.
I've rose to this occasion
to put you back into your place!
Listen closely, I'm anointed and
that is something you can never come against.
You understand that?

The dirt you tried putting on my name
will turn to mud and be put on your head.
You're a low-down dirty shame!
What you did was so foul and lame.
I can and will eventually forgive you of your sins,
but understand I have what it takes to win.

117

You might as well get out your violin now
because I'm putting all this to bed.
Rock a bye baby...
you just rocked yourself to sleep!
While you're doing that,
why don't you go choke on those false allegations!

A Letter to My Future Wife

I remember speaking you into existence.
You came into my life and
made my dreams become a reality.
You're a pleasure that I deeply treasure.
There are no measures or barriers
for the love I have for you.
God assures me with divine hope.
But with you, He gave me all
the security I'll ever need.

There is none like you.
You're so precious and pure.
I never wanted to pressure you,
but that same pressure makes diamonds.
You are that one...my beautiful diamond!
You sparkle with radiance, grace, and anointing.
You wear your crown like
the royal queen that you are.
I'm so proud of you and to call you, my wife.

I'm glad to give you my last name
and everything else.
I truly am in awe of you.
You see into my soul with your
fascinating and piercing eyes.
It's like you reach down into my heart
to pull out gold nuggets I have hidden inside.
You see me for the good qualities I have
in despite all my dirt.
Being around you never hurts...
it's so rewarding.

The love you give me is so warm,
inviting, and welcoming.
I only want to shower you with
that same love even more!
You deserve it all!
You're special in every way and
I thank you for being my best friend, my partner,
my counselor, my angel, and my soulmate.
The stars have now been aligned.
You're like the sun that kisses me
and makes my life brighter each day.
I love you always to the moon and back!!!
I thank God for you.

Need I Say More

There is a saying that goes, "isn't love grand?"
Does it always have to be a grand gesture?
What about all the little things.

The little things do matter.
So, let me ask you this...
When you decided to love,
did you even take a stand?
Or were you just playing in the sand?

Love isn't a sandcastle.
You build love by making a strong foundation.
What is your foundation?
Did your love withstand all the attacks against her?
Did your love stand the test of time?
Did your love prevail?
Let me unveil my love in this poem.

My love is special in every kind of way.
My love looks so good on the one that it's meant for.
My love is a sweet fragrance to the welcoming air
My love is more valuable than diamonds, rubies,
silver, gold, or money.

My love is brilliant. It is quite resilient.
My love is unbreakable.
My love is unshakeable.
My love is like thunder to my sweet love's lightning.
My love pours heavy like rain.
My love is bright as the sun.

My love is intense.
My love is strong and enduring.

My love is the answer.
My love has a swagger.
My love penetrates like the dagger that pierces the flesh.
My love is insatiable.
My love is nourishment for the soul.
My love has an appointment with destiny.

God promised me a divine meeting with Him,
the Creator of Love himself!
His love is unparalleled.
His love is fulfilling.
His love is the answers to my prayers.
His love makes a way for me.

His love is my miracle.
His love is my protection.
His love is my direction.
His love brings me joy.
His love is powerful.
His love makes me sing His praises.
His love is untouchable.
His love is unbreakable!

His love is forever...
it was the same yesterday, today,
and forevermore!
Need I say more?

A Whole New Love

Can you find a place in your heart to love me?
I have a special place in mine just for you.
I made a request to God through prayer
to find someone like you.
I've been waiting patiently for you.
I've been expecting you.
Am I welcome inside the walls you've put up?

My walls came crashing down
as soon as you came on the scene.
I know you're in rebuild mode...
but just know you don't have to do it all by yourself.
I'm here to help you baby.
I've been under reconstruction myself,
but I'm much better than I was before!
I know you don't need me necessarily,
but I feel like I'm more than useful to you.
I don't need you necessarily either,
but I invite you into my world
because I see you as the best part of me.
You're a blessing!

Don't you know that I love you so?
Don't you know that I'm for real?
I can't force you to pick me or
to even make you love me.
I can only hope you trust me enough
to take care of your heart.
I'm responsible and I believe I can handle it.
My heart pumps hard for you.
It bleeds so much love for you.
If you need more evidence,
see my tears that run down my face like a waterfall.

I want to swim in your tears of love
and dive deep into the depths of your soul
and discover the deeper meaning of true love!

My lady, have no fear!
I'm with you in this thing all the way til the end!
I make a covenant with you
that is unbreakable and everlasting.
God is our witness...
let us declare what we both know to be true!
There is no need to hide it any longer!
Even if it's a small, still voice...
I just want us to hear it from each other.
God will most definitely hear us,
but we also have to hear what He
has to say about this as well.
His voice is the most important to hear
and we must follow that calm and reassuring voice!

For most of my life,
I've wrecked almost everything that came my way.
This time...I'm not letting anything wreck
what we have together.
Baby, just hold my hand and
trust that we can get through anything together.
You built a hero inside of me.
I became a superhero because you believed in me.
But at the same time, I see a superhero in you too baby.
I believe we can fly and soar to even greater heights.

I would love to spend sleepless nights with you
on wonderful and exciting adventures.
I want to show you a whole new world.
A whole new me. And a whole new love!!!

124

Matador

I'm like a matador...
life is the bull that always charges at me.
If we reversed roles, then I would say
life has definitely got the better of me most of the time.
I tried to take life by its horns
and hold on for dear life.
I held my own though.
I'm still here, right?

I'm built for what comes my way.
I'll tell you; I have faith
not knowing what's behind the matador's red cloak.
I just go forward and rarely do I ever look back!
Sure, I've taken my bumps and bruises and took a few "L's".
But I kept coming back for more!!
I wanted to score victory because I believed it was mine!
I was determined and hungry for action.
I knew the best was yet to come!

My future is bright because
God has been with me all this time!
Now that I think about it,
I believe God may have been the true matador
teaching me a valuable lesson.
He brought out the best in me
and He was in control of the outcome!

Puzzle

The world is a big jigsaw puzzle,
it has many parts and so many pieces.
Its broken but can also be whole
if all pieces fit and can be unified.
Puzzles are intriguing to me.
Most people like me enjoy the challenge
of putting them together.
It's a brilliant exercise for the mind.
You can concentrate on being a critical thinker
by solving the puzzle.

Puzzles are unique and its truly a game of wits.
Relationships are like a puzzle.
The only difference is you are dealing in pairs.
Pairs have connections just like the pieces
that come together to make the puzzle.
Attraction leads to a conversation.
A conversation leads to an understanding between the two.
An understanding leads to a connection.
A connection leads to intimacy.
And intimacy leads to a sacred bond.
You see how all that fits together?

Our bodies have bones that are individual pieces
to make up our whole structure
known as the skeletal system.
But when you're the muscular, respiratory,
circulatory, endocrine/immune, digestive,
nervous, and reproductive systems...
you almost a whole person.
The only thing that could be missing
is the spirit of the person.

God breathed life into us,
and we are made in His image.
God is a Spirit who is also known as
The Holy Spirit that dwells within us.
When we die, our spirit departs from our bodies
and reunites with God.

Life is a puzzle that doesn't always make sense from our perspective.
Jesus is the missing piece of the puzzle!
Some of us look at things from a "piece to a whole" outlook.
Others, look at things from a wholistic perspective
and like to break things down into pieces.
In other words, some of us have a telescopic view
or a microscopic view depending on how one chooses
to make sense of things around them.

The beautiful thing about a puzzle is that it's a mystery.
Some things are hidden in plain sight,
we might need to investigate a little more.
Maybe look a little bit harder.
Don't try to make pieces fit
where they have no business of being fitted to.
Your schedule may not "fit" with someone else's schedule.
As much as you may want to be with that person,
that person just may not be a "fit" for you or vice versa.
Maybe that job field you're working in isn't quite a "fit" for you.
Perhaps that shoe you're wearing isn't quite a "fit" for you.

Puzzles don't compromise,
they all work together for the good like Romans 8:28.
I'm a piece to a puzzle, but I'm a whole person.
Sometimes I wonder where exactly I fit in the grand scheme of things.
I know there is a place for me somewhere. I'm sure you have all had
these thoughts at some point or another. But I tell you get in where
you "fit" in. Just remember that God saw "fit" to put you in His plan
to give you a hope and a future. Jeremiah 29:11 That's the puzzle!

127

Love Was in the Air

She got an angel face, but oh those devilish thoughts.
Don't mean to clip those pretty little wings of yours.
I would just rather you dance with me tonight.
I want to feel your rhythm and
be close to you for as long as I possibly can.

You're a temptress.
If I didn't know any better, I'd think you were an actress.
I can see you laying on a mattress
trying to seduce me with your sweet lies.

You're forbidden fruit.
I can only receive someone
whose pure and good for my soul.
I don't think we can endure this
flirtation ship much longer.

You're a good flame.
But I realize that I gotta blow you out of my life.
It's hard, I know...I know.
Its best to have you be on your way and
I'll be on mine.

It was fun while it lasted,
but all parties must come to a pleasant end.
Our chemistry was unlike no other
but we both know we were so wrong for each other.
I remember the scene of the crime
of where we first fell in love.
I'll miss kissing those beautiful lips for the first time
and especially for the last time.
The spell has been broken and
now we are free to go our separate ways.

Farewell, my love. I'll never forget you.
Remember me baby.
My love will stay with you forever.
What we had will always be enchanting.
Inhale to exhale...
now we can both breathe much easier
because love was in the air!

Safe Place

Everywhere I venture, I try to find a safe place.
I've been on the run for quite some time.
Trying to get cover from the enemy attacks.
I have valiantly fought in foreign and domestic lands,
but I now find myself wounded in the battlefield of life.

I need a place of refuge.
I need a place of healing and solitude.
I need sanctuary so that I don't end up in a mortuary anytime soon.
I'm just being real.
I am not bulletproof, but I'm wearing my vest of transparency.
Maybe you'll hear my pleas for help, or you'll ignore them.

Remember, God is with me.
He loves me and will help me.
I am seeking for a heart that loves me.
I would like my future wife to catch me in her arms
and hold me close.
I need her to be there for me.
I've always been the type to be the hero,
but this time I need my she-ro to comfort me.

I have been alone for quite some time.
I've been long isolated from my sweet destiny.
YOU...It's always been you that I needed to find.
I found your heart and you find mine.
Our hearts beat together as one.
Surely, God has blessed me with you as my safe place!

Parts of Me

There are parts of me I can't show...
parts of me I won't show to just anybody.
You have to be brave to be completely naked.
Shame and condemnation for too long
have been some things I've clothed myself with.
I want to be comfortable in my own skin and
most of the time I am...I really am.

However, once exposed most people can't handle
the unattractive scars that you carry.
There seems to be no empathy for hell
you go through in your life most of the time.
You often get looked down upon for your imperfections.
But name me one person in this world that is absent
from having any imperfections at all in their own lives?
Don't worry I'll wait!

Yes...I'm flawed but I'm working
to become the best version of me as we speak!
What I hold deep inside of me is valuable.
Why should I just give it away that easy?
There are best parts of me and there are the worst parts of me.
But one fact remains is that I'm a whole human person.

Sometimes I have parts of me
that seem to be scattered somewhere.
They are lost by the blowing of the wind.
Like an ocean, sometimes I get carried away.
Other times I float on what is left to my own devices.
Hurts have sunk deep down to my inner most bowels.
I want to let them out, but I'm too constipated.
If I let out the shit I've been holding onto for so long,
I bet most people couldn't stand the smell of it.

I'm sick and tired of puttin on a front to protect my heart.
I'm sick and tired of being lonely.
I'm sick and tired of being the way I am.

There are parts of me that people will never understand.
There are parts of me that even I won't fully understand.
There are parts of me that are healing.
There are just parts of me that you should not need to know
or ever want to know too!

Like a donor, I can choose to donate my body parts to science.
There have been times that I've lent my body parts
to sexual intercourse or vice versa.
I've realized that not every woman
is worthy of my great instrument.
Every part of me belongs to me.
But honestly it belongs to God.
Do you understand that?

So, for my farewell...
a part of me will leave
a promising legacy
for future generations to come.
And that's the part I can truly show!

Panty Dropper

Pay attention to what I'm telling you right now.
I need your full attention!
Listen and watch very closely.
I'm the master of ceremonies tonight...
I am your host known as
"The Master of Foreplay and Seduction."
Please follow my instructions.
Sit back and relax.
Close your eyes, don't open them until I tell you to do so.
You're my eye candy. You're also my arm candy.

There is no escaping this moment.
I'm sweet on you! I'm gonna taste you and enjoy the flavor of you.
I can't resist what melts in my mouth.
A lick here, a lick there. A nibble here, a nibble there.
Now I'm on your neck. Let me introduce my lips to your jugular.
That's the spot I'll be on regularly.
Making sweet love to you is my favorite scheduled episode.
I love watching your reactions to the power of my tongue
and my talented fingers.
I enjoy delivering thrills that eventually lead to plenty of spills.

Baby, just chill just settle down...it's just me and you!
You know I'm giving you the pleasures you like.
Bite down on the luscious and succulent lips.
I wanna make you shout and scream.
Let me hear you one time.
Actually, make all the noise you want.
I don't care whose around.
The neighbors are gonna hear a soundtrack
like they never heard before.
Tell me your fantasy, let me fulfill it with that ecstasy.
This isn't fiction by any means.

133

Our imaginations have become a sure-fire reality tonight.
I'm giving you all I got, I have plenty more in reserve.
I'm trying to hit that nerve!
You got curves of a goddess;
I navigate your body length like a highway.
I may go the distance for a certain amount of time,
but there will be some pit stops along the way!

Baby, I'm trying to take a toll on you
just like you're doing to me.
Falling in love is no accident,
but I'll say I've crashed inside your walls
at least this time around.
Neither party is at fault, no charges were filed.
But we do have a case of being horny.
The bedroom is my courtroom.
Baby, I'm your judge and your jury.
I can drop your charges like you drop those drawls.

You could have been arrested for
trespassing on private property.
But I escorted you back to my place.
I know you are seeing flashing lights
and hearing sirens right now.
I pulled you over only to bend you over,
because you know I'm an undercover brother
that will show you the kind of evidence
to prove that I'm a suspect in this crime scene.
I never fled the scene. I'm still here.
You can arrest me with those eyes
and captivate me with your sweet love.

You want the D! Show me how you'll work for it.
Show me how you'll beg for it.
Show me how you'll hurt for it!
And please show me how you'll sweat for it!

The love we make is a special treat.
It's hard for either of us to want to retreat,
we don't have a desire to surrender!

We have lives we must go back to.
We were in each other's custody while it lasted.
No hostage situations took place...well maybe just one.
We probably could break the law,
but instead we just broke the bed!
Until next time, this will be a night
I will always remember!
This was a panty dropper!

Pearls

Pearls are the most valuable treasures
outside of diamonds or rubies
The late, legendary musician Prince sang a song called
Diamonds and Pearls.
At this moment, I'm speaking to you about pearls.
Pearls are not your everyday common jewel you come by.
They are precious, expensive, attractive,
round, luxurious, and special.

Pearls come from oysters.
Basically, a clam that hides a treasure known as a pearl.
The world is literally our oyster.
Pearls can be found in the unlikeliest of places.
Sometimes you must go deep to the ocean to find them.
I see beautiful women, young and
old who wear them for decoration.

They are symbolic for fertility, grace, purity, and perfection.
It also represents hidden knowledge or wisdom.
Pearls also offer protection and are quite stylish.

In the Bible it's been quoted to
not cast pearls before swine.
(Matthew 7:6)
Because if you do, they will trample
those pearls under their feet.
Meaning don't offer what you hold dear
to someone who won't appreciate it.
Swine means pig and if you give your pearls to a pig
then they will get stuck in their snouts!
I'm just giving you pearls of wisdom, use it as you wish!

Speaking of pearls of wisdom,
I believe there are 5 types of pearls
a man and woman possess.
They are:
1) Your Wisdom
2) Your Wallet
3) Your Private Parts
4) Your Hands
5) Your Heart

Always protect them at all costs!
These pearls you have are very powerful and special.
They are investments and resources,
don't waste them on just anyone!
Enjoy your pearls while you still can
and don't lose them all!

Harvest of Love

She was like a plant.
She needed to be cared for and given plenty of attention.
I'm like an animal, I am on a hunt and I'm hunting for love!
We both have needs.
I want to plant seeds in a special person's heart.
I'm hoping that something will grow
and bloom into a beautiful blessing.
She may not want to give me any hope,
but little does she know that I would give her so much more!
I truly adore her! I can't ignore her sweet presence
and I just want her to acknowledge my existence too!

I know I have a bad habit of wanting to rush things sometimes.
But I'm learning to exercise patience...
it's not always easy for me but I'm willing to wait.
Sometimes when I talk to her,
I ask myself Why Am I Talking? (W.A.I.T.)
I can speak to you with my eyes and
that should reveal what escapes my heart.
I have the eye of the tiger!
My eyes can definitely communicate
to your eyes what you mean to me.
I try to hide these emotions sometimes.
But I have the courage to let my tears flow down
to the peaks of my dark cheeks without warning.

I can see that she needs healing and that she wants to grow.
It's a process for her. I know it can be hard for her.
Trust me, it goes both ways.
I don't know all her roots, but I can see that she is rooted
in a firm foundation of the faith.
I think she's in a good place. Or maybe not.
She may not be in a place to give anything right now

or make any promises.
But understand this,
God will give you the desires of your heart.
He will even do the same for me.
I believe! I hope you can believe that too!
I'm not someone who gives up very easily.
But there comes a time you must let go.
Take things slow. Let things flow and take their natural course.
Like a river, nothing stops the current...
it gets through obstacles and moves into the places it needs to be!

Kind of the way the heart pumps blood
and circulates it to different parts of the body.
I may not be what you desire.
But I know what I've acquired.
I'm definitely an acquired taste for sure, but I know I'm good.
Maybe I'm good for you...or maybe not so good either.

However, I know that I'm crowned with God's unmerited favor.
You are too! He knows me from the inside out.
He knows you just the same.
I confessed my truth with these words and my mouth.
But with that same mouth,
I delight, rejoice, and thank God for you!
You'll always be beautiful to me...
keep growing and keep blooming!
As for me, I'll wait for my harvest of love will come.
My seeds of prayer will be answered,
and I have peace in knowing God will deliver.
And all is well within my soul.

Acorns

Its fall season and I see a bunch of acorns on the ground
that have fallen from the trees.
I always admired the acorns I saw.
I knew the squirrels enjoyed gathering
and feasting on them as often as they could.
Acorns are a delicate food source
that is collected by certain animals for survival purposes.

We can learn a lot from what these animals do with these acorns.
Acorns are like currency...
we try to get as much of it as we can
because they are valuable to us.
Acorns are saved just before winter
so there is enough food to last through the blistering cold weather.

Acorns are nuggets of wisdom
we get to share with people.
Acorns also can be shared with us too...
Acorns have a hard exterior wall,
but you must find a way to break through to get all what's inside!
Acorns are treasures that shouldn't ever be taken for granted.
You're getting a really good treat when you encounter an acorn.

I love when trees are adorned with acorns...
it's nice to see them drop in on us every now and then!
When I see them, I'll be sure to pick some of them off the ground.
Not sure what I would do with any of them but
keep them as a reward for myself.
But I don't mind sharing any of the acorns wisdom
I've gained from them.
Thank God for acorns!

Poetry That Became My Wine

You're like poetry that I can't ever seem to get enough of!
You're the poetry that I enjoy writing about.
You're the poetry that I enjoy singing about.
Baby, you're the poetry that I dream about.

You're the poetry that is music to everyone's ears!
You're the poetry that turns on my fire and desire!
You're the only poetry that I require.
You're the poetry that keeps me going.
You're poetry that became my wine!

Pool Party

Its summertime, it's hot outside...
let's have a pool party.
Don't worry, I'll send out the invitations to everyone.
The pool party that I'm throwing is going to be a big,
very fun special occasion.
I need all the beautiful people to come
and hang out with the host with the most.
To plan out this party, I'm going to need some help.
I need someone to help me with decorations.
I'm trying to give off a cool summer/Hawaiian vibe, you know.

I need all my folks to pitch in on a party.
We need food, drinks, floats, music, and games.
Most importantly, we need all sexy women in bathing suits
and bikinis to attend this party, you dig?
Rules for the party is no drama,
leave that shit at home.
We don't get down like that at my spot!

You can bring guests but please don't bring any lames.
Bring your own beer!
Appetizers, music, and sunscreen will be provided.
Bug spray is highly encouraged.
Party starts at 3:00 p.m. and lasts until whenever.
There will be dancing of course, and we will have a dance off!
This is a private event and there will be no kids allowed.
Adults only!!!
Come over and let's have a good time.
RSVP to come to the best pool party of the summer!!!

Bikinis To Beanies

I feel a sudden change in temperature.
Brrr...the wind is blowing something cold and blistering.
Seasons change like a new pair of drawls.
I had to Fall for Winter and be engaged to Spring.
After that I got married to Summer.
After the honeymoon was over, I took it to the streets.
Then I got tired of that shit, and I went undercover.

Me and my boo got boo'd up and
went under some covers to keep nice and warm.
Cuffing season at its finest.
But I can't help but notice that
we've gone from Bikinis 👙 to Beanies now!
I'm not complaining.
I enjoy seeing a little exposure and
bringing it back to a bit of mystery again.
The freaks come out all year long.
Tell me if I'm wrong.
Don't worry I'll wait!

When you're in the dating scene,
you can go from hot to cold or vice versa.
People you deal with nowadays are like chameleons.
Eventually they'll show you their true colors.
I've never skied a day in my life,
but I'll hit the slopes to get myself a snow bunny! 🐰
But I sure do miss the bikini season though...
I wanna play in the sand box with one of these summer hotties!
Shots are all on me for this one!
But I'm not afraid to shoot my shot either.
Oh, shots fired!
Ladies you know you need to run for cover.
I'm single and ready to mingle.

I know how to jingle those bells around Christmas time.
I'll be your mistletoe all through the year.
I come bearing gifts.
Make sure you bear your good fruits!
I'm not scared to indulge in some freaky shit!
I'm always on the move.
Don't get caught off guard.
I'll make my presence known and felt.
I'll make all your hearts melt.
I'm always ready to see some
Bikinis to Beanies!!!

More Than What You Are

In a world you can be anything,
why would you be less of who you're meant to become?
Don't rob yourself or others of the gift you possess inside of you.
To my ladies, don't be eye candy...be soul food!
To my fellas...don't be lazy or complacent,
take responsibility and be great!

Geographical location doesn't determine
the kind of success you'll have.
But your psychological position always will.
Don't be afraid to leave the shore,
the worst you can do is sink or swim.

Follow your moral compass
and be led with truth and conviction.
It's not where you're from, its where you're at.
You'll fall into traps of deception,
seduced into schemes and
introduced to several universal themes.

In a world where it's essential to separate
the real between the fake.
Not everything will be a fair shake,
be prepared to get shook.
Don't worry and have no fear,
you have what it takes to succeed.
Each experience equips you for
the very moment you're facing now.
Encourage yourself and
face your inner demons.
You have the ability to demonstrate
the amazing power inside of you never knew existed.

Stop acting like you don't have nothing to offer.
Step up to the plate
be confident in the swings you take
at what life throws your way.
Sooner or later, you'll hit a home run.
You got this. Believe it!
You're built for this.
You were created to be so much
more than what you are!

Masterpiece

Truthfully, I don't have much to give to you.
But I can bring you the treasures of my heart.
I loved you from the very start.
Every moment with you is priceless.
I know at times we need our space which is fine
but understand that absence makes the heart fonder.
I often wonder how much closer we can ever be.
I really don't want to be anywhere
other than right here with you.

I feel safe in your presence.
I find comfort in your loving arms.
Your love disarms me completely.
I melt like ice cream on a hot sunny afternoon day.
I don't wanna sound corny or cheesy,
but with you I can be easy.
I feel ok just being me.
But honestly its always gonna be about us.
I know you value my love and
that you accept it as your only currency.
We are worth each other's investment.

Our love is a true testament
of standing the test of time.
God has been our anchor
when we have faced fierce and turbulent winds.
We navigated through the rough seas of this life
but only because God was on the ship with us.
Many times, we could have drowned in our sorrows
and fears of tomorrow.

Yet we've overcome the storm.
It passed over us and we were welcomed

with a rainbow  of opportunity.
The sun greets with a happily ever after
and the moon is our spotlight.
We bask in the glory of love.
It rejuvenates us and brings us so much joy.

Once upon a time I was searching for a ship mate.
Many days I was lonely and lost at sea.
I hurt so bad because I thought all hope was lost.
God brought us together and
we found each other through Him!
I thank God for you, and
I thank you for being my everything.
You are the best choice to have as my wife.
I don't regret it either.

I adore you more than you could ever know.
I cry because you lift me up when I was weak.
You were my voice when I couldn't speak.
You were my eyes when I couldn't see.
Like Celine Dion,
I'm everything I am because you loved me!

Thank you for taking a chance on me.
You won't ever regret having me
as your loving husband.
I cherish you all the days of my life.
Now and forever.
You're an answered prayer and
my angel that will always be with me
until the end of time.
I believe I see a piece of heaven
when I gaze into your eyes.
I was blind but now I see into the future.
It's filled with promise and blessing.

If we took our last breaths together,
I know that we were compatible
like Adam and Eve.
But only this time we want to l
earn from their mistakes.
We both know what is at stake.
We are each one another's conduit.
We give each other what we each
require and desire.
Love brought us together and
we are God's loving masterpiece.

Life Designer

The Creator had it on his mind
to create this wonderful creation that exists today
one that we should take time to appreciate
while we are still breathing.
He spoke this world in existence...
He started it off with saying it was good.
Then he ended it momentarily when
His Son, Jesus Christ was dying on the cross
He spoke His last words, "It is finished."
But you know He had to return to glory
to be with His Father to rule and reign
until His kingdom comes again.
When God finally says it's a wrap, it'll be a wrap!

So, while we are still inhabiting this planet,
take a look around and marvel
at His grand and spectacular work!
God is a true artist that made
a broken world His masterpiece.
He literally made us live in color...
He created diversity and distinction.

Nothing keeps us separated from Him
and His beautiful imagination.
His plan for us is literally a stroke of pure genius.
He goes well beyond science and art...
He is a life designer!
His Word is the foundation,
and His touch makes everything come into complete order.
There is no design that compares
to His divine craftsmanship.
He is the architect of all the wonders in this world!
It's hard to comprehend or explain how great God truly is.

He is above the hierarchical system
because He is the King of Kings.
His influence overshadows any pandemic,
idea, idol, problem, difficulty.
God loves us all and I believe that
He loved the finer things in life.
We are His most treasured possessions.

He put His seal upon us.
He marked us with His amazing love.
His Holy Spirit is the label that he fashions us with.
People around the world can witness
the anointing that we are adorned with.
He gave us our imprint and we should be proud
of who He made us to be.
We are made in His image.
We are His imagers.
We are meant to reflect His loving nature.
He gave us the Master's touch...
in His eyes we are the apple of His eye!
May we love our Creator
all the much more as He loves us!
Let us celebrate the Holy One,
The Almighty God...
our wonderful
LIFE DESIGNER!

Perfect Picture

I've seen so many pretty pictures...
just so many pretty pictures all around me.
They all have their own allure,
but one thing is for sure...
there is one I have my eyes set on.
There is something so special about her.

She is above all the rest as far as I'm concerned.
But what makes her so different than anyone else?
I'll be glad to answer that one for you.
I get a twinkle in my eye just thinking of her as we speak.
As I'm writing this love letter,
obviously, she would have to be the envelope to it.
My  is the stamp that makes it all official.
I am sending her all of my love
I hope she receives it in time.

My beloved showed me how first class she could be.
She showed me how much of a masterpiece she truly is.
She is my truth to all lies that have surrounded me.
She is the understanding to my wisdom.
She is the push to my go.
She is the warmth to my embrace
the smile that she puts on my face.

I rest easy at night when she
lays her head on my chest.
She is master to my peace.
She makes my heartbeat faster than any rap song.
I love singing her praises...
when I am feeling low,
she lifts me up with the high notes of her love.
When I was defenseless, she came to my rescue.

When I was lost, she found me.
When I was in the fog, she gave me so much clarity.
She is the ⊙, ☾ ,and ☆'s.

I'm the shadow that is by her side.
I'll be there for better or worse, til death do us part.
I love her with all my soul.
She is the missing piece to my puzzle.
She is divine, beautifully. and wonderfully
designed just for me.
She is my Mona Lisa...
She is a treasure that is worth more
than diamonds and pearls.
If I could, I would give her the world and more.

She is the better half of me.
On behalf of me,
I present her with the gift of unconditional love.
May she cherish it and much as I cherish her.
All of me just loves all of her.
Nothing compares to her in the slightest bit.
She is tailor made to fit me.
She is my best friend. She is my rib.
She is my loving partner. She is my wife.
I thank the LORD above for her all the days of my life.
Together we make the perfect picture!

I'm happy

I'm happy being me.
I don't need a clone to duplicate
my face of expression.
I light up with joy when I wake up each morning.
It's always something new and
exciting to look forward to!
I embrace the now and what's to come.
My past has come and gone,
yet I won't forget what it taught me!
Or where it brought me!

People may not understand why I'm so happy.
That's ok! They don't have to know.
My joy comes from my Father in Heaven.
He created me in His image.
I'm called to be His imager.
Like all His creations,
we are all His great bundle of joy!
I love the way God made me...
He made no mistakes.
He put so much detail into me.
I turned out the way He imagined
I should be and nothing less.
He did the same for all of you.
Embrace your uniqueness.
That's your defining quality.

Whoever doesn't accept you,
that is certainly their problem and not yours!
Show yourselves love and compassion.
Don't be so hard on yourself.
We are all His wonderful masterpiece!
He is the Artist of all artists...

He is the Master of this production!
He gets all the credit for what He has done!
He deserves so much praise and more!

I'm happy He brought me from a mighty long way.
I'm happy He protected me in foreign and domestic lands.
I'm happy He lifted me up.
I'm happy He remembers my name.
I'm happy He fed me.
I'm happy He gave me my identity.
I'm happy I make Him proud.
I'm happy He made me a part of His family!
I am happy He loves me and forgets me not!
I am happy He gave me tears to cry.
without them I wouldn't be human!

He knows my heart 🖤 and I often cry
I'm overwhelmed with such joy in my heart.
You can be happy and cry at the same time.
I cried out to Him so many times
He always came to my rescue.
He never left me or forsaken me.
How can I not be happy?
He gave me a smile to share with the world.
Not just any smile either...
when I smile just know that
He is smiling at you too!
I'm so happy!

Peace

Where can I go to find peace?
I am weary, frustrated, and worried
about things in my life right now.
I've had some doubts and some fears.
I'm burdened and just feel worn out.
I need to rest, maybe that will help calm these nerves.
Sleep is good for the soul but
strangely that doesn't give me total peace at all.
I'm still restless. I know I need a vacation.
I deserve a nice getaway from all the chaos going on
but where do I go?

Maybe I'll go to the mountains
or head to the beach.
I probably will go to Clearwater Beach
or check out the Blue Ridge Mountains.
I can remember reconnecting with nature
and clearing my mind from distractions.
I shut my phone off
take in all of my surroundings.
I may sit and do some riding
to gather my thoughts.
I may take a walk and
get my exercise in for the day.

Eventually, I'm going to have to come back to reality.
Vacation is over!
We're still dealing with all the insanity
going on in the world.
I know that to achieve true peace
I have to accept myself as I am.
I have to learn to accept things as they are
if I can't change them.

Peace ideally comes from the Prince of Peace.
My Lord and Savior Jesus Christ,
He calms and restores my soul
after I lay everything down at His feet.
In Matthew 11:28, it says come to me all of you
who are weary and burdened, I will give you rest.
Peace is available to us all and it is truly a gift.
We can't absolutely experience true peace
until this world passes away
God returns to bring His Kingdom to Earth.

Take heart, take joy, and take peace
God has overcome the world and we can too!
Pray for peace, live in peace,
be at peace with your neighbor.
When the enemy tries to come for you,
call on the name of God and say peace be still!
Jesus commanded a storm
to be at peace and be still while
He was sleeping on a boat with his disciples.
When we die and depart from this Earth one day,
we will all rest in peace.

The Villain

Meet the villain.
He or she is always portrayed as the opposition,
antagonist, or the bad person in every situation.
Villains are depicted in such a way
that defines their behavior as sinister or evil.

In every story there is a hero that almost always
must contend with a villain.
Villains add an interesting dynamic to every plot.
Sometimes we are so biased in that we think
the hero always needs to be seen in a good light.
We often forget that that our heroes have flaws
just like a villain does too.

Some villains didn't start off bad.
Obviously, something traumatic or
life changing happened in their lives
for them to transition into the character that they have become.
Some villains have suffered a terrible or unfortunate fate.
They must live with the consequences of their choices or reality.

Villains most of the time are usually hurt people
that try to hurt other people.
Villains often seek power, fame, revenge,
retribution, incredible or satisfaction in
making other people's lives miserable.
Villains rarely show any compassion
to those who may be suffering.
Villains more often than not, will push their agenda
and not care about anyone but themselves.

Villains can be considered a hero's arch enemy or nemesis.
Believe it or not, villain's need heroes
to bring out the best in them. Villains have no morality.
Equality just doesn't exist to them.
Villains are people we must learn
to have compassion for.
Sometimes villains are misunderstood
for whatever reason.

Villains have mental health issues
that are inflicted upon them as trauma.
Villains are their own worst enemy and
they usually fall because of their pride or ego.
Villains prey on weak-minded people
and take advantage of them.
Villains will always have to battle
not only the hero but also themselves too!

There is always a villain in somebody's story and
sometimes I've definitely been included in that category.
I'm sure we all have at some point.
I can truly say that I've played the role.
Maybe I'll get an Academy Award like
Denzel got for Training Day.
To be honest, I don't want to be the villain.
But I admit that I've been perceived as a villain
a few times in my life before.
I don't see myself in that light at all.
I strive to be the best man I can be.

The villain is presented as a challenger
to the hero and vice versa.
Villains are powerful and have committed many crimes.
They love to cause mischief! They also love to cause a scene.
Peace and justice try to intervene
in a world of chaos created by the villain.

The villain always has schemes and trying
to cause turmoil everywhere they go.
Like Scarface, say hello to the bad guy...
it's the last time you'll see a bad guy like this,
let me tell you!

Apology Tour

I just want to take this opportunity
to share my heart with you all.
I haven't always done right by most people.
I didn't always say the right things either.
Sometimes, I would just react and
didn't use much common sense.
I never claimed to be perfect.
I'm not an angel even though I wish
I could have their wings to fly above my mistakes.
I never enjoyed making other people hurt.
I was going through my own kind of hell,
battling my inner demons,
trying to keep a peace of mind all at the same damn time!

I realized that hurt people truly do hurt people.
If you ask me, the whole world needs therapy.
I don't wanna play victim here, I just want to let every person
I ever hurt, said anything bad about, or mistreated...
that I am very sorry, please forgive me.
I am better than what I was
I'm striving to be a better man every single day.

I want to make things right between us.
I know it may not happen overnight,
but it's a start in the right direction.
I'm more mature now that I was back then.
I did some really stupid things that I'm not proud of.
I think we probably can look back on some things
and have a laugh about it.
Maybe or maybe not...
I'm not trying to make the past irrelevant,
I just think we can move forward and start fresh.
No need to keep putting logs on the fire

unless we are roasting some Smores.
I know you don't want to keep burning forever
I am not trying to get burned by you either!
It's not easy to always admit when I'm wrong,
but I take full accountability and responsibility for my actions.
Back then my ego got the better of me,
but today I am more humbled than I ever was.

I've learned some hard lessons and
I don't plan to keep repeating the same mistakes.
I have decided to go on this apology tour
because I want us all to live in peace and make amends.
There will be scars but through God's miraculous healing
and love we will be able to mend and go beyond the pain.
Like Ruben, this is my Sorry for 2020!
My apology tour has officially ended.
I hope you accept this as my token of my love
and giving you the best me I possibly can!
Apologies Matter!

I Left My Heart in California

Somewhere along this journey of mine,
I left something that keeps me going back in California.
I left my heart  in California....
I left a place that I called home.
It's a place that there is a thin line
between love and hate.
I'm proud to be from there,
but I dread going back there at the same time.

Bittersweet memories are what I remember most about California.
California is the most famous place in the entire world.
People from all over travel to experience the golden state.
My time there had some golden nuggets of incredible experiences.
But I never seemed to strike it big out there!
Maybe I could have been three feet from hitting the golden jackpot.
I could have stayed but I needed to spread my wings
and expand to new horizons!

It wasn't easy for me to leave what I knew as home behind.
Truth be told, I miss it sometimes.
I miss the weather, my family & friends,
the attractions, entertainment, music, etc.
I remember there was a person I wanted so badly in life,
but it just never was meant to be in the cards for us.
She saw me as like "a brother"
never anything else beyond that.
I had to accept that.
She moved on and I moved on too!
But sometimes I wonder, what if?

But on the real, I've been reminiscing lately.
It's cool to imagine what it could have been sometimes,
but I laugh it off like "nah, I'm good now fam!"

I thought about her and for a split second and
wondered if she still thought about me too.
Then, I realized it's best to leave things where they belong...
in the past!
What didn't kill me made me stronger!
I could have held out a little longer,
but that would have been a terrible mistake.
I'm glad she's in a good place in her life
I'm happy where I am in life as well.

It's been several years, and
our paths have never crossed again.
Life is like a highway,
some people come along and ride with you for a while
but really, they are just passing through.
Other people are going in the same direction
seem to come along with you for the rest of your journey!
They are lifelong companions
that remain loyal to you and
are going on the same mission as you!

California is not going anywhere,
I know I can always go back to visit.
However, I'm the type of person that
continues to move forward.
Life is not a fairy tale and love is not like the movies...
my story is like a continuing saga
of twisted plots, turns, and sequences.
Stay tuned for what happens on the next episode of
I Left My Heart 🩶 In California!

Letter to my Sis

Dear Angel aka my baby sis,
I'm writing you this love letter
to express how much you mean to me
what it means to be your big brother.

I can remember when you were born,
how excited I was to have a baby sister!
Mom brought you home from the hospital
I was so happy and honored to be your big brother.
Seeing your precious face made me beam with pride and joy.
Like your name that was given to you,
you were heaven sent and an angel that blessed us all.
You didn't come here with wings,
but you always seem to know how to fly
above the chaos of life.

You always possessed a great imagination
and eclectic taste in culture.
I used to always play with you as kids,
sometimes I played a little too rough.
I got carried away when I would wrestle with you,
I didn't always know My own strength.
I felt bad when I would see you cry
I would tell you to dry your eyes
because I didn't want to get in trouble.

I could be mean at times,
but I was also very loving and protective as your brother.
You are always a daddy's girl,
I admired your relationship with your dad.
But honestly, I would be low-key jealous
of the bond you two shared.
Sometimes, I thought you were too spoiled,

but now I can see why you were always baby girl.
You never were shy about telling people how you really felt.
You are a true Gemini and
it's an honor to share the same birth month as you.
Together, we rule and celebrate our month of May.

We didn't always see eye to eye,
but I know that we both have
a deep love and respect for each other.
You got your own kind of personality,
your own kind of special vibe…
you got black girl magic and
always gets down for your tribe.
If I could describe you,
I would say your fierce, loyal, adventurous,
funny, strong, loving, and sensitive.
You seem hard on the outside,
but you're really a softy at heart.
I've enjoyed watching you become
the woman that you are today.

You had your setbacks and
lessons you learned the hard way,
but you always wised up and glowed up.
You're living your best life now and
I'm happy to see you get the blessings you truly deserve.
If you ever need anything, I'm always here for you baby sis.
I'll never stop being here for you.
If you ever need advice, Big Brother always got your back!
We're all we got and even though distance has separated us,
the love has never left.
There is nothing I wouldn't do for you.

We got the same mama and different daddies, we still family!
Blood will always be thicker than water.
You showed me love by being there for me or

picking me up when I was down.
You're amazing and you're an angel
because you're a messenger.
You're meant to fly, and your wings will never be clipped.
As my angel, you have touched me more than you realize.
Keep being who you are
and any man that is fortunate to have you
should know he's got a real one!
You're a keeper I'm not just saying that either.
Angel, you are a blessing and you're a sweetheart!
I'm proud of you sis, keep shining
I'll always cheer on my baby sis to the very end.
I love you so much!
God bless you always.

Take Me Back

Take me back I want to go back
to a time where things were simpler and more normal
I know this is a broad statement to make
so let me guide you with my pen
by driving home my point

take me back to my childhood
where kids actually enjoy playing outside
take me back to a time
we had family dinners at the dinner table
and barbecue cookouts in the park

take me back to when we had
Sunday dinner after church service
as weird as this may sound but
take me back to school
so I can learn all over again

take me back to when parents actually cared
enough to discipline their children
even though it was tough love

take me back to when music
actually was good and
meant something for people
from all walks of life

take me back to a time
when marriage was sacred and
vows were actually kept

take me back to a time where
we didn't have to rely on phones for everything

we actually use them
for what they were intended

take me back to when
movies were much better
than they are today

take me back when
going to grocery stores
were like exciting field trips

take me back to when
creativity took precedent
over technology

take me back to where
natural beauty was more
in style than plastic surgery

take me back when
kindness was received and
reciprocated rather than
being seen as weird or threatening

take me back to a time
where people would take
the time to get to know you
and invite you to their place or in public

take me back to a time
where dating wasn't so complicated
take me back to when
people would take the time
to pray with you and for you

take me back to when

law enforcement made regular visits
in our neighborhoods and
made people feel safe and secure

take me back to a time
we actually made hospital visits
to our loved ones
who were sick and terminally ill

take me back to where
love was in the air
take me back to when
men love women and
women love men

take me back to when
God wasn't taken out of school
take me back to a place
that isn't like what it is today.

Smell The Roses

I recently took some time out of my life and began reflecting.
I started realizing that my life has been a journey,
but I haven't always stopped to smell the roses!
What do you mean by smell the roses?
Well, that's a good question, let me explain.

You see my friend; your life is like a garden.
The special people in your life like your family,
friends or spouse are like roses.
Your achievements, blessings, finances,
and experiences are like roses too.
Sometimes we lose sight of the roses
we have gained along the way
to our journey in pursuit of purpose!

We are conditioned to always move forward,
set and reach new goals and achieve greatness.
We are always constantly working to
either please ourselves or someone else.
Sometimes you must pause and
smell the sweet fragrance
of what your life has offered you!

Life goes on but it goes by really fast!
Enjoy the roses you have received and
make sure you give others their roses too!
Everyone deserves a chance
to smell the roses while they still can!

Residents of Romance

I was a resident in your heart but
seems like I've become a stranger.
I was once a welcomed guest,
now I'm evicted from your love!
Did you raise the rent or something?
I thought we could both be under the same roof;
the proof says otherwise.

You already know,
I'm not going out like that.
I'm still at your doorstep
with a dozen roses in hand.
I look pitiful, but
you make everything beautiful.
I want a second chance.
We can fix this!

I still can be your covering,
there may have been some leaks...
but we can certainly patch things up with time.
Undo the latch and let me in.
I want to feel you and enjoy
being in one another's arms again.
I promise I'll never fail you again!
I'm so proud and glad
we are residents of a brand-new romance!

The Fuss Over Valentine's Day

The fuss over the infamous Valentine's Day!
The day where people catch this so called "love bug"
and want to be all up in their feelings.
In the past, days like this would make me so sick!
I never seem to have a side chick or a side kick...
I've always been the kind of guy who goes solo!

I know true love is a beautiful thing,
but nowadays people make love seem so casual.
Not much seems to be offered to the table as usual.
It's hard to serve any love when
you're not getting any of it in return.
Giving without reservation seems to be expected.

Yet reciprocity is rare to our human species.
Love is a gift, and some people treat it like feces.
Love naturally should never stink.
Oh, the aroma should smell so much sweeter.
I'm happy to see couples celebrate and love each other
but don't just do it only for one day out of the year.
Make it 365!

Singles, I'm aware that we are all we got.
I ain't forgot about us.
Our time will come but, in the meantime,
let's practice self-care and self-love!
You may get sick and tired of being lonely,
but honestly, we're never alone.
We are loved and cherished by God.

Remember, the best is yet to come!
Valentine's Day seems like it's all for show.
It's not a real holiday even though

many people celebrate it around the world.
It's all commercialized and often,
I always thought of it as a complete joke.

That's how I feel about it,
but don't let me reign on your parade.
Enjoy the festivities while you can.
Valentine's Day is not always roses
because most couples break up
before, on, or after Valentine's Day.
It's sad but it's true.
I've noticed some women getting together
with their girlfriends and celebrate
something "Galentine's Day!"
It's cute. Nothing wrong with that all.

Most guys might audition to be somebody's Valentine.
Some may actually be the romantic type.
And you got the other guys who
don't really give a damn about Valentine's Day.
Maybe because it doesn't really benefit them whatsoever.
On Valentine's Day you're spending money it,
but are you really getting anything back in return?
I'll let you all decide that.
It's a big deal to some people but not me.
I just don't get why there is always
a big fuss over Valentine's Day!

Independence Day

We have often thought about, talked about,
walked in something I'd like to call independence.
It was the year of 1776;
American independence was born
thanks to the Declaration of Independence
written by Thomas Jefferson.

Over the years, there has been a power struggle
and even a civil war for human rights.
Oppression has always been the arch
nemesis of independence.
Some things worth having are worth fighting for.
There is a cost associated with independence.
Lives have been lost and blood has been shed.

Independence required sacrifice, hope, and faith.
Independence is a gift that we should all appreciate
and not ever take it for granted.
Independence is a gift and
it's not meant for the entitled.
Independence is a majority victory for those
who are alive long enough to enjoy it.
It just isn't all about the fireworks
that light up the night skies.

We celebrate freedom across America today
and we all come from different walks of life.
Our country deserves nothing but love,
but we are more divided today than ever before.
Independence sparks passion, compassion,
unity, redemption, and love.

Independence means something to all of us
whether we like to admit it or not.
Now that we have independence,
let us not stop our fight to keep it.
Never lose your independence,
it's the most valuable thing we got next to love.
Happy Independence Day everyone!!

I Need Your Help

I'm not sure if I should ask you,
but I really need your help right now.
I've been struggling and burdened with something
that's been too heavy for me to carry alone.
I need some help and you're one of the few people
that I believe can help me.
I'm usually a very independent kind of a person,
but every now and then I need some assistance.
I don't have all the answers or
have everything all figured out. I'm not perfect.
I'm coming to you for some advice.

You can't trust everybody, that's why
I'm very selective on who I ask help from.
Like Debarge, I've had some problems,
and no one could seem to solve them.
But you are the answer to my prayers.
I'm not used to being vulnerable,
I've always known one way and that's to be strong!

Everyone has a story and
some stories just all sound the same.
I'm asking you to please hear my heart.
Sincerity and authenticity are not far removed from my soul.
Can't hide or run from the pain anymore.
Trauma is what I suffer from
but I'm working on a better way to heal.
I know I must surrender it all,
but it's hard for me to give up control.
No man or woman is an island.
We all need each other's help!
I know what time it is and what time I'm on.
There is no shame in asking for help.

I need a friend to lean on.
I need love and compassion.
I need to get off my crutches of pride, fear,
laziness, tiredness, resentment,
jealousy, and insecurity.
I need comfort right now from the
trials and tribulations I face.
I need to be refreshed.

Sometimes I feel lost and
can't seem to find my way.
I've prayed for help, and
I've been waiting on the LORD to hear my call.
I've poured out my whole heart and soul.
I don't know how much more I can go on like this.
I'm reaching for a helping hand,
so precious LORD take my hand!
I need your help!

My Responsibility

Everyone is responsible for their own sales in this life.
That includes me too!
As a kid in my youth,
I didn't have to worry about responsibility.
Once I became a teenager and began to know better,
I was given the daunting task of responsibility.
The word responsibility was thrown around a lot
by my grandparents and parents alike.

Taking responsibility meant taking initiative to do
something you said you would do or were expected to do.
It also meant that you were given a certain amount of trust
by someone or by a group of people.
Responsibility means you take ownership and
accept the consequences for your actions
or whatever is under your supervision or care.

Responsibility is accountability.
Leadership comes with a lot of responsibility
especially if you're an authority figure
it takes courage to take responsibility
regardless of the circumstances.
When you take responsibility,
you are refusing passivity essentially.
You must be intentional about taking responsibility.

Laziness just won't ever cut it.
Responsibility can give you credibility,
power, and respect.
I take it upon myself to have responsibilities
I won't allow anyone else to pick up my slack.
Unless they want to share the responsibility,
then I'm okay with that.

Outside of that exception,
I have a responsibility to take care of myself.
No one will take care of my needs like I can.
I have a responsibility to my family,
or should I say to the family I'll have some day.
I have a responsibility to work,
love, protect, and provide for them.

And lastly, I have a responsibility
to get myself in alignment
with God and have a relationship with Him.
I have many responsibilities,
but I'm willing to accept all of them
because I'm a man and
I have to do just that!

The Nerve

Have you ever heard the term, He/she got some nerve,
or this person is on my last nerve.
They sure is working up my nerves today!
We all got nervous systems that control
different parts of the body using the brain's functioning.

Nerves are sensitive and sometimes things can irritate
or cause stress to some individuals.
I know some of us have seen people do or
say the craziest and most outlandish things.
If we are honest, some of those people are us.
I think when we get the nerve to say what's on our minds,
people look at us like we have lost our freaking minds.

I've looked at people sideways too
for having the nerve to certain things that were uncalled for.
Some people are bold and have no filter.
Sometimes you just think that's just the way that they are
so we may give them a pass.
We might get a pass at times for
our inappropriate behavior too.

I prefer to touch a heart rather than a nerve but
believe me if I hit a nerve more than likely
that person had it coming!
A few times I probably had it coming too.
I think at some point in our lives,
we've all had it coming so we got what we deserved!

I got nerve to stand up for myself as a man!
I got the nerve to call you out on your B.S.
I give you permission to call me out on mine too,
but you need a clearance for that though!

181

Don't get outta pocket now. Lol.

Mental health is real and
a lot of people out there are having nervous breakdowns!
Our words can be sharp sometimes,
we need to be careful how we use them.
Words cut deeply and can draw fresh blood.
They cause wounds that may take a long time to heal.
Some might not ever heal.

Last I checked we all got a pulse.
Our nerves are steady working.
Don't get nervous.
Just keep calm and be careful of the nerve you may offend!
Some of ya'll might just be on my last nerve.
I may have the nerve to give you a piece of my mind.
Just sayin. So, Jesus, please take the wheel!

Reconciliation

You're looking at me with eyes that despise.
But I'm too busy keeping my eyes on the prize.
You fail to realize that I've exchanged my past for His future.
I'm not what I used to be so you better get used to the new me!

You staring at my plate looking at the scraps I was given.
Need to worry about what's on your plate and
find you a morsel of gratitude.
Before you do that, pardon me, while I say grace!
I thank the LORD for all He has provided.
I say a blessing over this food and
that we are nourished with the nutrients of it and the Holy Spirit!

We sit at the same table,
but my presence does not seem welcomed.
I embrace you like my brother or sister in Christ
even if I have to do so at a distance.
No hard feelings, we can still break bread!

I read somewhere in His word that said to love
your enemies and those who persecute you.
Since I'm part of His plan, that's exactly what I'll do.
If you feel you need to get to steppin, go right ahead.
We can walk this out, but that's entirely up to you and me.
I'm cool with it so feel free to decide.
Love resides in my heart because Jesus is the lover of my soul!
Truth be told, we are on borrowed time anyway.
Gotta make every minute count.
There is power in reconciliation
when our affiliation is with
the King of all Kings!!

Tensions

Tensions...there is so much of it in the air these days.
It's always been there.
I want to clear it up like clear skies,
but they remain like dark storm clouds.
Tensions bubbling like the passing of gas...
it doesn't smell nice at all.

Tensions are foul to begin with anyway.
Tensions blow like the wind sometimes...
like a boxing match, it can always go back and forth.
A jab here...another jab there.
Then after that comes a hook and before you know it
someone gets caught with an uppercut.
That's the extreme...but most of the time
tensions are nothing more than verbal sparring sessions!

Temperatures can get pretty hot, and tempers can flare.
Tensions can give bystanders quite a scare.
They can tear into you a Lion pouncing on its prey.
Tensions can go from being unspoken to all out animated!
Tensions cause discomfort, irritation,
isolation, sickness, and disease.
Tensions can bring a lot of attention.

It can be sensed and recognized with a quickness.
It's hard for it to be undetected or ignored.
Tensions can be seen going viral nowadays...
sometimes tensions can blow things way out of proportion.
Tensions can almost have you on the brink of war
like Cold War rivals, USA and Russia.
Tensions can go away with some diplomatic peace keeping or
they can remain like unforgiveness.
Sometimes, there is a sexual tension...

which can be awkward but
like an envelope it should be properly addressed.
Tensions should be mentioned without shame,
fear, condemnation, or judgment.
It's not a good idea to suppress it.
But there is a way to handle it...
you must deal with it! Tensions are real...
confront them with courage and
don't let them get the best of you!

Silence

Silence is peaceful yet deadly at the same time.
There is a time to speak,
but there is definitely a time to listen and be silent.
Silence is a golden opportunity to meditate and
enjoy some solitude and clarity.
Sometimes, I just have no words.
I may not have the strength to utter the words I should say.
I don't always feel up to entertaining people with my breath
or words...for me, it's like what's the point.
I don't think I should even waste my time.
I may not necessarily want to always share my thoughts
with strangers or people I even know.

Silence can be crippling and used as a handicap
when you might need to speak up.
Silence can be misconstrued or interpreted as fear.
Silence is rarely seen as a sign of strength.
Bravery and courage don't always have to be
loud or even boastful.
Sometimes it takes on a whole new meaning.
Sometimes it showing you have
restraint or power under control.

Noise can be annoying, but to some people
silence can be just the same.
Challenges are meant to have a response...
but silence can truly speak volumes.
Silence can demonstrate great wisdom and
not show everyone the hand you're playing.
Silence is calculating and even clever.

Silence can give you leverage,
and it can definitely work in your favor.

Neutrality is seen in a negative light.
The world tells you to pick a side,
yet it's hard to choose
going against your values or morals.

So, you may remain in neutral territory
therefore remaining silent.
It's like trying to choose between
your mother and father.
Silence can be seen as avoidance.
As we have seen in recent times,
silence can be used as a sign of protest.
Calling Colin Kaepernick.
Silence can definitely cause tension.
Unspoken words become words that our eyes
will speak out very loud and clear!
Our eyes can communicate how we really feel.
Eyes can't hide our emotions.
Everything comes to surface eventually.
Silence may be your safe haven, but at some point,
you have to respond to something in life.

Nights can often be silent.
Yet the stars are silent, but
they cause us to react or respond to them.
I can't speak for the world, but
I can speak until I no longer am able to.
When I die, that is when
there will be complete silence.

I Need a Hug

Attention please!
I need a hug. Like seriously,
I really need a hug right now!!
Sometimes, we all just need a hug.
No words, just a hug.
I know you probably aren't the
type of person to be touchy feely.
But let me say this, hugs are like
the most comforting and
one of the nicest things you can give to someone.
Hugs are a blessing, and
they should never be taken for granted.

Hugs mean a lot to people and
sharing an embrace is an intimate exchange.
Hugs symbolize hope and bring encouragement
to those who feel despair, hurt, fear, trauma,
frustration, affliction, hopelessness, etc.
Hugs are warm, caring, and loving.
Hugs can be given at any time and
the best part of it all is that they are free of charge.

Hugs are welcoming and they can
also be a way to say goodbye!
Hugs having healing properties and
they can close the gap in distance or separation.
Hugs can be given in reconciliation and in celebration!
I am a hugger and I'm not afraid to admit that!
Hugs can save lives and uplift people
that are facing dark times.
Hugs are a form of love and are token of kindness.
Hugs are open invitations and
are a safe place for people to seek refuge.

Hugs can last a few seconds to a lifetime.
I've been through a lot and I need a hug.
I need a hug from the future love of my life.
But most of all, I need a big hug from my God
because I'm leaning on His everlasting arms!!!

Belong

I have searched for so long for a place
where I might actually see myself belonging.
I have been through familiar territory,
but places I've been don't seem to welcome or embrace me.
Sometimes it's just me. I don't fit in with everybody.
Can't associate myself with just anybody.
I often can feel like a nobody,
but I know I'm somebody even if I'm different.
I have been on the path of isolation
seeking my final destination.

I don't belong on the street like the homeless.
I don't belong with the lost.
I don't belong with the thugs.
I don't belong with the inmates.
I don't belong with the hypocrites.
I don't belong with negative people.
I don't belong with liars and cheaters!

Most people are like characters that belong on stages.
There are some interesting theatrics
that are performed in the world
that Shakespeare called a stage long ago!
Puppets belong on strings,
but creation belongs to the Creator.

A lot of people desire freedom,
but often can't seem to get out of their own way.
Mental prisons are not good for our mental health.
We don't belong in a place of darkness,
confusion, rage, or shame.
It's a dungeon that keeps us
from reaching our full potential...ENLIGHTENMENT!

Confinement restricts us from freeing ourselves
out of the traps of deception.
We need reassignment to
find ourselves to redemption!
Some people think they belong in chaos.
But order belongs in our lives.

The need for acceptance is something
the human psyche craves.
People tend to starve for attention and validation.
What we don't realize is that we don't belong in everyone's
inner circle, and they don't belong in ours.
It's ok to be different or unique.

People may feel the need to critique you,
but it doesn't really matter what they say or think.
You may even feel the need to critique others
but honestly what you think or
say doesn't really matter either.
You may not be everyone's cup of tea
and they may not be yours.
What you can try to do is get in where you fit in.

We are not meant to live in a bubble.
We need to get outside of our comfort zones
and seek to learn about diversity.
We all come from different races,
different places,
and have different faces...
but one thing we all have in common is
we all belong to the HUMAN RACE!

We don't need to qualify to be something more,
we already are what we need to be.
We need to just BE...
Be you and be more than you ever dreamed of.

In a world full of do's and don'ts...
just do your best to be a good human being.
We all belong, but the truth is
we just need to figure out
how we can all get along.

We have gotten it wrong so many times,
maybe one day we'll get it right.
We suffer long in this battle of long-suffering...
we are more than conquerors
that belong on the battlefield of life!
Do you know where you belong?

Power Struggle

Sitting here watching this election,
votes from everywhere are getting counted in every state.
America as we know it is in a very sad state.
We are more divided than ever.
It's come down to color. Blue or Red.
Media footage gives biased views to its viewership.

This country seems to thrive on division
because it brings so much confusion.
America seems to enjoy chaos but despises order.
We fuss. We fight.
We cut people off who think differently than we do.
We disassociate ourselves with those who see the world
from a different lens or perspective.
People always yelling out "facts"
yet don't practice any sort of tact.

We want justice. We want change. We want equality.
But all people do is piss, whine, and moan.
Get over yourselves. Grow up!
Stop trying to make yourself seem
more important than you really are.
It's not about you or me...
this is about seeing the bigger picture.

Yes, we may have our differences but
let us align ourselves with truth, love,
morality, faith, and hope!
One man becoming the president doesn't mean
he's going to save the world.
He's human just like we are.
The world already has a Savior and
the government rests upon His shoulders.

You already know I'm talking about Jesus.
C'mon somebody!
He still sits on the throne.
Ballots are being counted,
but Jesus already had my vote long before this election.
He is the ultimate authority.
He willingly shares His power with elected officials,
but nothing about His power is hierarchical.

The president is given limited powers for a season.
May we support him and pray for him during his presidency.
However, there are checks and balances among the
Legislative, Judicial, and Executive Branch.
They are balancing systems for each other.
We are all pieces on the chessboard.

Jesus is the true King and Judge.
He can always bring the world to its knees.
In the end, every knee must bow, and
every tongue must confess that He is LORD.
Now that's what I call checkmate!

Weight Watchers

My weight tips the scales, but that's nothing new.
I've always been a big guy.
There were times I tried to be thinner
but my hopes of that lately have become slimmer.
I've lost weight before but gained most of it back.
No question I've slacked.
But it's so irritating to hear all these so called
"Weight Watchers" talk about health yet
they put down overweight people.

You give no encouragement or very little reassurance
to help those who struggle with their weight.
You wonder why so many people give up.
You wonder why so many lose motivation.
You wonder why people commit suicide.
Insults are so quick to be directed at someone or
a certain group of people.

I've learned to live in my skin and have an extra thick skin.
I'm proud of who I am, and
the most important thing is I love myself.
I'll admit people are right to see me as a big man.
But I'm more than just my weight.
I am an all-true man...
I'm not measured in pounds.
I'm measured in heart and soul!

Pound for pound, I am the best all around.
I'm a heavyweight and I'm champion that
dominates any opposition that comes my way!
People love to throw verbal jabs...
but just let you know,
my jab is much stiffer, you'll feel my power!

And I'm not talking about physical either!

A lot of people wish they could be my size.
My value doesn't go down because of my weight,
I'm still grown and sexy.
Any woman lucky enough to be with me,
would be more than satisfied.
There is just that much more of me to love!
I got all the love to give.

So, next time don't judge me by my weight,
judge me by my character!
There is more to mee than meets the eye.
I surprise a lot of people and
I usually make people eat their words!
Get your weight up and
stop being a weight watcher!

Good Hair

It's been said that a woman's hair is her glory.
A woman is essentially her hair,
and her hair is what makes her a woman.
Women from all cultural backgrounds
are noticed primarily for their hair.
It's not always a fair assessment
to judge a woman by her hair.

However, the way she cares for her hair
tells quite story by first impression.
The way a woman wears her hair is usually dependent
on the mood that she's in for a particular day or occasion.
Some women and even men
obsess over having good hair!

There are many hair styles worn throughout this world.
Hair is unique and can draw attention in good or bad ways.
I believe that hair requires some maintenance,
and it should be taken care of as much as possible.
It's a struggle to have good hair.
Not everyone can be Becky with the good hair!
Hair is a form of art, and you do with it as you wish.

Hair care matters to people!
I know hair can get messed up and
the elements can really do a number on your hair.
Hair needs your attention.
It needs vitamins and it needs to be combed.
It should be groomed and look healthy.

I know some people may not have any hair or
may have lost some hair due to stress related issues.
Just because you don't have hair today,

doesn't mean you can't have hair tomorrow.
You can cut your hair and eventually it will grow back.

In my case, I've never had long hair,
so I always get it cut short.
I always go to the barbershop
to get a fade with a chin strap.
But I have recently grew out
a full beard on my face.
I wanted to look more masculine
because when I was younger,
I barely grew a mustache.

Some people wear dreads on their head.
It's a cultural phenomenon that originated
from places like Africa and Jamaica.
It's widely popular and is associated with
Caribbean music and Reggae.
I never wore dreads but, in my opinion,
I don't think it would fit me honestly.

To each their own I always say.
You also have permed hair that people like to wear.
Perms require a lot of work.
You must press the hair with a hot comb,
condition the hair with a relaxer
and some other chemicals.
Women wear perms but
men have frequently worn them too!
For me burnt hair stinks...
the odor is quite strong for my nostrils.

You have people with curly hair.
You have people with straight hair, wavy hair,
braided hair, a bob, a weave, nappy hair,
pigtails, short hair, and more.

Hair has variety but it comes at a cost!
It's not cheap to keep good hair maintained.
It's one of the reasons a lot of people like
to cut or chop off their hair.

Sometimes hair can just get in the way
or become too out of whack and
it's necessary to get a good trim
every now and then.
Hair keeps the scalp warm but,
in the summertime, it can make you feel so hot!
Hair can be both a gift and a curse.
Sometimes hair grows in the wrong places
and other times having good hair
makes you more than satisfied.

Hair comes with preferences.
I prefer my woman to have long hair.
I am attracted to beautiful hair,
but I also like some short hairstyles too!
One that comes to mind is Halle Berry's short hairdos.
She looks amazing with it and
I can tell she is proud of her hair.

I definitely want my woman to be proud of her hair too!
Women usually have a habit of playing with their hair.
I want to run my fingers through my lady's hair
to feel the texture of it.
But I know some women
don't like you to touch their hair.
Hair is definitely sensitive for most people.

I care about hair. Good hair is self-care.
Hair brings me joy.
Hair that turns grey is a sign of wisdom.
Samson's hair was a source of his strength in the Bible,

but he lost his strength when Delilah cut off his hair.
The hair sits on the head like a crown.

For me, hair is royalty!
Every hair on our head is numbered by God.
Like Willow,
a lot of people like to whip their hair back and forth.
I remember the Jheri curls back in the day,
that was the original drip!
And of course, you cannot forget about the Afro puffs!
The original symbol of black power!

Man buns have been popping up
all over the place these days.
Some people opt for the ponytail
and it's very low maintenance!
Let your hair down and let it flow.
Be careful not to pull back on it
unless you don't mind that kind of treatment.
Be good to your hair and it will be good to you!

Don't Panic

Don't panic, I got this!
You got nothing to worry about cuz
your man knows how to take care of this situation.
I'll show you how I get shit done!
I'm not afraid to take control and risk it all.
I'm ready. I'm your protection and you can rest assured
that I'm gonna see us through.
You're probably thinking
how exactly am I gonna do that?
Well, my answer is simple.
By trusting God because
He is all divine, powerful, faithful, all knowing,
all telling, all mighty, all truth, and all loving!

I submit to His authority becuz
I know God is the one who
is in complete control of everything!
Nothing surprises God.
God fears nothing.
God worries about nothing.
God has no doubts.
God is undefeated!
In God in whom we trust,
whom shall we fear?
Don't panic baby,
God has equipped me to handle
what I need to handle.
But God is the answer.
He is The Way, The Life, and The Truth.
He is the True Vine.
God will surely take good care of us.
He promised us that He would, and I believe Him.
You should too!

201

Acceptance

Why can you seem to accept
Visa, Mastercard, or Express but not me?
I got currency and I am definitely
someone who knows their worth.
You can take that to the bank!
I'm anything but deficient,
I'm better than your average!
You treat me like minimum wage.
At this stage in my life, I'm an investment.
I'm safe and secure.
Nothing is insufficient on what I can supply
to a fine woman like you.

You accept the bullshit from other men
who aren't willing to invest in you at all.
You settle for less when you could have so much more.
Don't underestimate what I bring to the table.
Baby, I'm stable and oh honey, I'm truly able
to satisfy someone like you.

I never declined to give you any sort of attention.
But I guess you weren't paying any sort of attention
to the signals I was giving you back.
I deposited my interest, but you withdrew
and gave me the cold shoulder.
I was bold enough to step to you and
give you a breakdown
of the portfolio of my character.

I know you have plenty of other options, but
I need you to open your eyes
to see that I'm the real deal.
So why don't you tell and show me something good.

I thought we could do business and
mix it with some pleasures you might like!
I applied and appealed myself to you, but
you look at me like a fraud.
I was saving my best for you.
But you're to blind to see a man with a plan.
You would rather have options. I understand.

You don't want to be tied down
until you know it's a sure thing.
Go ahead and do you then.
You chose to default and
go back to what you're used to or familiar with.
The window for what could have been,
is now closed.
I always wanted some acceptance
but it's hard to find these days.
I don't want it from just anybody
but from a worthy person that is willing
to take a chance with someone like me.

Acceptance is a token of appreciation.
I want to be appreciated but also respected.
I know with acceptance
you need some sort of insurance.
In other words, you need protection.
Some of us crave that more than acceptance.
I yearn for acceptance all that much more!

I don't like my plea for acceptance to be ignored,
it's a real need that I have for my own security.
I have my insecurities just like everyone else and
I'm not perfect by any means!
All I want is someone to make the right decision
to accept me for who I am, and
I will accept her just the same!

203

However, I realize that I'm already accepted and
approved by God the Great Accountant and
Lover of My Soul!
I am sealed in His glory forever. Amen.

Dating Today

Dating is like waiting for an acceptance letter
at a so-called Ivy League College. 😊😊😊
Some people claim to be the best of the best
and they only take what they think are the "best."
Sometimes they aren't offering much of anything.

Just being real.
No matter what your credentials are,
you always have to pay a tuition before
you ever get offered any kind of a scholarship.
You rarely get by just walking-on.
Sometimes the person you have interest in will
WALK 🚶 ON by you and not even give you a second look.

Standards are high for someone like you, and
you should earn your way to that person's heart.
No doubt about it.
But anyways, you get interviewed by these great
"board of directors" who are more than likely good friends
with your person of interest.
They huddle up and discuss if you're actually "dating material."
A decision is made and if they like you,
you'll be welcomed with open arms.
If not, then there's the door and you can see your way out.

There are no guarantees in dating. It's like rolling of the dice.
Sometimes you get lucky and other times not so lucky.
Meanwhile, you got competition that always tries to one-up you and
do whatever it takes to get in good with this Ivy League princess.
Some guys jump through so many hoops for women
like they are in a circus! 🎪
Over here looking like a bunch of clowns.
Most guys try too hard and end up on the denied or

declined list by this person of interest.
Sorry guys, you didn't make the Dean's List!

Yet, that same woman will go ape
over the next baboon she sees and
inside it has to drive you bananas!
Keep your head up though, you're still winning.
You're not defined by this setback.
You'll be accepted by the right one that's meant for you.
Unfortunately, this one ain't it for you.
The best is yet come.
A door will open or better yet,
you can just leave the door open!

Compliments

We all have received a few compliments
in our lives at one point or another.
It's a really good feeling when you hear them
and when you're open to receiving them.
The definition of a compliment is
a polite expression of praise or admiration.
I've been complimented many times over
and I'm very appreciative of the ones that I have received.

The best compliments are the ones you never quite expect.
I enjoy giving compliments as much I do getting them.
Compliments are like candy...they are very sweet,
but they lose their flavor after a while.
Sometimes people hear compliments so much
they get used to it and get bored of them really fast.

Some people see giving compliments as a form of "ass-kissing."
That could be true in some cases,
but the way I see it is I'm giving people their flowers
while they can still smell them.
Compliments very much make a difference
in someone's life. Compliments are a great reminder of
how awesome or appreciated you are.
Compliments are positive affirmations
and they set the tone for any interaction.

You don't lose anything by giving someone a compliment.
It's a nice way to demonstrate kindness to each other.
The antonym for compliment is to insult or criticize.
Compliments make us realize just how special we all are.
Compliments bring me joy and others around me joy as well.
We live in a world where people seek a label called validation.
Which can have a bad stigma attached to it.

I think people have a need for acknowledgement,
acceptance, and recognition.

Humans thrive on compliments.
I compliment beautiful women not only about their looks
but also, their personality and intellect.
I'll compliment a guy if he has on a cool hat,
watch, or car he's got.
I'm confident in who I am.
I'm not ashamed of giving compliments whatsoever.
Compliments should not be considered "creepy"
if it comes from a good place.

Ladies, if a man takes the time
to give you a compliment just say thank you!
Fellas, if a woman takes time
to give you a compliment just say thank you!
From my experience men usually give
more compliments to women than vice versa.
When you're attracted and interested in dating someone,
you typically ask the person out.

Obviously, you have to approach that person
and you introduce yourself.
And you probably will follow it up
with some nice smooth talk
and give that person you like a nice compliment.
That person can take interest or reject your advance.
Compliments aren't only meant for romance.
They can be used at any time.
Compliments are great icebreakers.
But don't overdo it! And don't over think them either!

Whoever I date should see me as a compliment to them
and I should see them as a compliment to me.
Make no mistake, no one is entitled to a compliment

but it's a good gesture or courtesy to build up others.
Compliments can be engraved in people's minds...
they never forget how a genuine compliment made them feel.
You're welcome, compliments of Aaron Woodson!

Kick Rocks

You had my approval, but
now you have been terminated from my life.
There is no renewal... no explanation is necessary...
Your services are no longer needed.
Situations expose people and
as a result, leads to a dismissal or removal.
I really wanted this to work,
but sometimes things just fall apart.
Should have recognized the red flags,
but somehow, I let you slip through the cracks.
You can't build on a weak foundation.

There is no resolution for half-assed effort,
disrespect, abuse, and infidelity!
Being single is my solution to this problem.
You can be held responsible for your actions,
but I hold myself accountable for this whole mess...
never again will I put myself in this kind of situation.
I'm ready for a new equation...
addition by subtraction is my new attraction.

I don't need a fraction of your affection...
I got my own satisfaction!
You're no longer my distraction!
Now, I can focus on these transactions!
I'm starting a new company called Moving On.
My empire is run only by me.
You were a client and you've been sent on your way...
by the way, I'm the man with the power now!
You can't touch this!
Now kick rocks!

Life is Love...Love is Life

Life as we all know starts in the womb.
The mother's womb is a safe place for a baby waiting to be born.
Sperm meets egg just like boy meets girl
or man meets woman.
Pregnancy is a blessing
so why not give infancy a chance.
Mothers have a choice, but what voice
do you listen to when you make your own decisions.

Ladies, you carry a gift, but you also have a choice.
I know it can be complicated deciding
to bring a child into the world
knowing that you've been raped.
It's hard when you've been forced
into a situation that you had no control over.

Life's not fair and like Willow Smith
just whip your hair back and forth.
I know you're confident
you're making the best choice for you.
Emotions run high when your mind
and heart are battling for ultimate supremacy.
Intimacy lit the candle, and
you seem to be burned out on both ends.

I understand it's a lot for you to handle.
I'm not here to criticize or condemn you.
I know people judge you
for doing what's unpopular.
You have the right to be the authority
but remember who's the priority!

Life is precious and valuable,
something we all should be thankful for.
Our lives were paid on the cross.
When Abraham was about to sacrifice
his own son Isaac, God told him not to kill his son
and there was a ram caught in the bush
to be used instead.

God is prolific in every sense of the word.
God is both pro-life and pro-choice
even if you choose to have an abortion
or did so already doesn't mean
God will love you any less.

Let's not stress over man's ruling and
may we comfort the mothers that struggle
with their decision they have to make or carry out.
We have all fallen short,
but regardless of the outcome
God still gets the glory for your story.
There is beauty for ashes.
Just remember,
life is love and love is life.
We love you.

Rabbit Hole

At some point in our lives,
I would think we've all heard
or been aware of the term, "rabbit hole."
I'm sure you're thinking of the animal
and yes, rabbits do happen
to dig holes for themselves as shelter.
There is absolutely no way to know
how far down that rabbit hole actually goes.
We can only assume it probably goes pretty deep.

The actual term "rabbit hole" that I'm referring to is referred to
is defined as, "a completely bizarre or difficult state or situation
conceived of a hole into which one falls or descends.
When adults are engaged in a conversation
or debate about a topic,
they tend to argue their viewpoints t
hat can often lead into a rabbit hole.

The flow or direction of the discussion can lead
absolutely nowhere and there is no conclusion to the matter!
You can literally spend hours or
even days dragging on about a subject.
Sometimes, we think there is a logical explanation
for everything and of course we want to be right!
Things can sometimes be darker and
deeper than what we actually know.

If you think you're going to go down a rabbit hole
and magically pull out a rabbit...
I say good luck because chances of that
ever happening are very slim to none.
Sometimes, we even dig ourselves a hole
that we can't seem to get out of.

Rabbit holes are slippery slopes,
and they can be very tricky
or complicated to deal with!

We can also go down a rabbit hole
assuming things about people
we have absolutely no knowledge of.
Rabbit holes are tempting to explore,
but they are not very inviting either.
If you're stuck in a rabbit hole,
get out as quickly as possible.
Don't bother even wasting your time!

I'd rather jump in a foxhole,
than a rabbit hole any day of the week.
Stories that are told can often have holes in them,
but we're not detectives unless
we personally do that line of work.
Rabbit holes are mysteries and
can present endless detours.
Stay on your path and
leave those rabbit holes alone!

Triggers

Triggers...what are triggers?
One definition would be the pulling of a trigger on a gun on a firearm.
There are some people out there who are "trigger happy."
They love or have a tendency to pull the trigger
for any unnecessary reason.
Sometimes, those same people are scared, so they react by squeezing
the trigger of a gun or an assault rifle one too many times.
Before you pull the trigger of a firearm or rifle,
something first would have to be triggered in your mind.
A thought stirs up in your brain before it begins in action.
We as humans have a fight or flight response to
any traumatic events or episode.

Adrenaline is a contributing factor to human response and high
stress situations. For example, I am a military veteran, and I was
deployed to Iraq (Middle East) and while serving my time there I
was in hostile territory. I was safe with the military personnel that
were deployed with me.
However, there were some tense and
uncertain times that triggered things in my spirit.
Before I joined the military, I was one way,
but as soon as I got out, I knew that I was different.
It was hard to admit that at first.
Times change and people change eventually.
Some memories take us back to a place we don't even
want to think about sometimes.
We have nightmares, panic attacks, fits of rage,
or setbacks at random times.

Even childhood experiences can haunt us into our adult adulthood.
Conflicts in relationships, divorces, financial problems,
and more can be the match that lights the fuse.
Sometimes medications can trigger some things in our body

that isn't compatible for what you're prescribed.
Even a bad joke can be just enough to trigger someone to react
in a threatening, aggressive, or violent manner.
Bullying can make victims retaliate or continue taking the abuse.
Lust, greed, jealousy, selfishness, defensiveness, neglect,
anxiety, depression, and anger are all destructive triggers
if not properly addressed.

Some triggers can be chemical biological and physical.
For example, the cause of a volcanic eruption is when enough
magma or melted rock builds up in the magma chamber,
it forces its way up to the surface and erupts!
The act of sex or intercourse triggers arousal or
hormone or hormones!
Also, ejaculation often occurs at the end of intercourse.
Love triggers deep intimacy within couples who engage and are
intentional about loving their partners.
We all have triggers, and our triggers are our responsibility.
It isn't the world's obligation to tiptoe around you.
We can't choose what happens to us, but
we can control how we react to it.
Be aware of your triggers, but
there is no excuse to let them get out of control.
Deal with your triggers people.
Don't shoot yourself in the foot!
Keep them triggers on safety!

I Know the Feeling

Oh wow....I had no idea you were going through this.
I'm very sorry to hear that.
My heart goes out to you.
I know the feeling.

Have you ever been engaged
in those kinds of interactions?
I know I certainly have.
So, let me tell you I know the feeling.
I know the feeling when
someone walks out of your life.
I know the feeling of heartache.
I know the feeling of guilt.
I know the feeling of shame.
I know the feeling loneliness.
I know the feeling of sorrow.

I know the feeling of losing a loved one.
I know the feeling of sacrifice.
I know the feeling of worry.
I know the feeling of failure.
I know the feeling of uncertainty.
I know the feeling of hopelessness.
I know the feeling of being of being so confused.
I know the feeling of being used and abused.

I know the feeling of being disrespected.
I know the feeling of being upset.
I know the feeling of embarrassment.
I know the feeling of getting rejected.
I know the feeling of being in denial.
I know the feeling of having trust issues.
I know the feeling of being tired.

I know the feeling of not
feeling like you're good enough.
I know the feeling of betrayal.
I know the feeling of being perceived as the villain.
I know the feeling of being persecuted.
I know the feeling of being sick and tired.
I know the feeling of feeling like a fool.

I know the feeling of trauma.
I know the feeling of pressure.
I know the feeling of vulnerability.
I know the feeling of not feeling appreciated.
I know the feeling of falling in and out of love.
So, trust me when I say I know the feeling!

You Never

You never gave me a chance.
You never made the effort.
You never listened to me.
You never were honest with me.
You never loved me...like ever!
You never trusted me.
You never believed in me.
You never understood me.
You never admitted when you were wrong.
You never remembered special events or
celebrations that took place in my life.

You never defended me.
You never admired me.
You never helped me.
You never encouraged me.
You never saw the best in me.
You never valued me.
You never prayed with me or for me.
You never laughed with me.
You never laughed at my jokes.
You never shared your secrets with me.

You never looked at me the way I looked at you.
You never would communicate with me.
You never had much to say.
You never told me where you were going
You never wanted a future with me.
You never gave me we what I deserve.
You never said sorry.
You never would ask me if I was ok!
You never visited me in the hospital.
You never wanted to grow.

You never wanted to compromise.

You never wanted to go to church with me.
You never wanted to meet any of my friends.
You never wanted to meet or spend time with my family.
You never wanted to make love to me.
You never wanted to pay for anything.
You never saw me as your type.
You never accepted me for who I am!
You never wanted to have a child with me.
You never wanted to marry me.
You never told me you cheated on me.
And mark my words,
you'll never...never...NEVER
see or hear from me again!

Salty

Have you had something that was a little too salty?
I know I've had a few things I've tasted
that was too salty for my liking.
Food should have the right amount of seasoning
which happens to include salt.
There is another kind of salty
that's common these days.
People can get this symptom known as being "salty."
I'm no stranger to it myself, but
I try to be a cool customer as much as possible.
Some people are extra salty,
and they really have no reason to be.

Salt is a substance that should be used with discretion.
Words should be sprinkled with salt.
Kinds words that is.
It's not fun being around salty people...
they just seem too bitter for their own good.
Salty moods are not my kind of vibe.
But on the other hand,
sometimes people have a right to be kind of salty
if they are rubbed the wrong way.
Salty is the opposite of sweet...
but it's a close relative of sour.
The faces people make when they're salty
doesn't look pleasant at all.

However, it can be comical to see sometimes...
sometimes folks just need to relax.
Use some bath salts and make a bubble bath.
Take their salty behinds in there and just chill.
Get over your saltiness and
stop being so salty!!!

Nothing To Do With You

Most of the ladies that ever came into my life
never really gave a shit about me!
You want to know why, let me tell you why.
They only wanted me for what I possessed,
they never wanted just me.
I wasn't good enough for them unless
I had the money, the power, the status, or the fancy cars.
They ignored the star that I already was
until I became a brighter one!
I've always shined, but their vision was dim
and blurred like Moonshine.

They wanted the sky but never valued the star....me!
It's not easy to find a man like me.
I'm one of a kind. I'm not like any other men.
I'm built differently. I'm the rubber that meets the road
and like Ford I'm built tough.
I've had enough of these women wanting only test drives.
They never can stay for the full ride.

I come fully equipped.
I know I got some miles on me in this life,
but that doesn't mean that I hold any less value.
Cars depreciate over time but being a good man does not!
Most of these women don't want good men.
They are energy suckers that bleed men dry.
They think they are entitled to everything men worked for.

G.T.F.O.H. You wonder why some men become maniacs.
You're no good for our souls.
Most of the time you like to ghost guys whenever you feel like it.
You love to tease and get mad when we begin to chase.
You walk around like you're the definition of perfection,

but you're just as flawed as "us" men are!

I try to give these women the benefit of the doubt.
I let a lot of shit slide but when I speak up,
I get bad attitude vibes!
I can only be me and I like me.
I'm not changing a damn thing about me.
I'm only doing me from here on out.
I gotta be true to my character.

If these ladies can't see me for what I am
then they don't deserve me period!
I'm worthy of respect.
I'm not entitled,
I just expect to be treated
like a king not a peasant!
If you want to settle with losers,
be my guest but do not come back
in my presence ever again!
I have nothing to do with you!

Push Through

Society tells you that you must do more to succeed.
People say they want to see you grow,
but most of them really don't.
They hate on you for being average and
they hate on you for succeeding.
But when you fail,
they want to kick you when you're down.

I am the type to get resurrected
every time I fall or get knocked down.
I can't go out staying down and defeated.
I was meant to taste victory and triumph over all the odds!
People think I'm odd, maybe I am sometimes.
Regardless, I know that I am an overcomer,
and I am unstoppable.
I am suited for greatness
and built for the best yet to come!
If people can't see it, then they are truly blind.
The right kind of lover will see me for who I am,
and she will see me as her champion.
I have grown leaps and bounds
but I must continue to keep that pace.

Life is not slowing down anytime soon.
I'm prepared to go the distance!
I'm ready to go. I'm ready to bring it!
I am enough and I can do all things
through Christ who strengthens me!
As long as I have Jesus,
I will always succeed because
He exceeds expectations and changes
atmospheres with His awesome power!
So, in the meantime just push through!

Trying My Best

I don't always have to be first.
In fact, I don't even want to always go first.
But I'm selfish to some people if I go first.
To others, they think I'm too aggressive or
in some moments I am perceived as not leading.
They tend to think I'm passive or timid.

When I follow, I just want to listen and learn.
But then I am asked to speak
when I don't really have anything to say.
All I really want to do is grow.
But here is the thing, growth hurts like hell!
I'm not interested in winning every battle
but I'm not backing down either!

Sometimes, I feel allergic to the people I'm around.
They could feel the same way about me.
Whenever I find myself in isolation,
I can find temporary solace.
But I find myself in sort of a hiatus
because I've stayed in retreat mode to protect myself.
I realize I have wounds that need to heal.
I can't let the enemy steal any of my joy.
I emerge from the darkness and
gracefully walk into the light!

Even in my weakness,
His grace is more than sufficient for me!
The only one who should be first in my life is God.
Followed by others and finally myself.
However, I struggle with the battle between
what I reveal and what I conceal.
I just want to keep it real.

Am I the only one who feels like this?

Surely, not...please be gentle with me,
I have a very tender heart.
I don't always get off to a great start,
but I definitely know how to finish!
I want to finish well.
I'm vulnerable, but I'm brave.
I know I have work to do.
We all do.
But please know that I'm trying.
I really am trying my best!

They Don't Get It

I've always been my own kind of man,
my own kind of boss.
If they don't like me, it's their loss.
I got my own shit to deal with.
I'm not about to give them free attention.
What I look like a sucka? GTFOH.

They got to earn their way into my life because
I'm not giving any of these women a free pass.
I'm the prize and it's time they realized that.
Not trying to be full of myself, I just know what I'm worth.

These women don't seem to get my leadership,
personality, charm, humor, or conversation.
I'm an amazing guy with plenty to offer.
I'm built differently.
These women have no idea
what I've been through to get here.
It took a while to get me here and
I got my foot in the door
and I'm not going anywhere.
I'm not gonna waste my time.

I'm not gonna entertain these birds any longer,
they don't see how fly I am and how high I can fly!
Like MJ, all I can do is sigh.
I know I'm not every woman's favorite
curriculum but so what?
I stand out and I'm designed to challenge mindsets.
I'm very interesting, I'm far from perfect...
but I'm also not boring either!

One day they gonna learn or maybe they won't.
Enlightenment will someday meet curiosity and
something beautiful may actually happen in my life for once!
As of now, I have nothing to prove.
I'm making progress and ascending to greater heights.
Someday I'll be famous!
If they don't get it now, they'll never get it!

The Cry from Within

Sometimes, I don't know if I should laugh or cry...
when I'm laughing all I really wanna do is cry.
Tears fall like rain down the peaks of my face.
Sometimes, I need my space, but
what I really want is comfort and compassion.
Life is full of so many distractions
as I try to lose myself in this cold world.

I've participated in a few war campaigns,
yet the toughest war that I fight is from within.
Love is what I seek in healing...
but I'm internally wounded.
My scars don't show on the surface, but
if only you could look within the depths
of my soul to see them for yourself.

The past is dark and ominous,
yet my future looks bright...
it's like a tug of war between the two.
The present is cloudy at best...
but I pray for a breakthrough!
I'll admit, I may be in trouble sometimes...
but I know who can save me!
My precious Savior, Jesus Christ!
He hears my cry from within!

Wrote Up a Storm

Words from my heart has spoken things into existence.
I won't pretend like the best hasn't yet come,
it's here and it's here to stay baby!
These words I write are embroidered into your conscience.
They are designed to make you feel some type of way.
My metaphors are in fashion like Christian Dior.
But if I'm really honest, I keep it all the way Gucci.

Stanzas stay on deck like Tesla,
I move like a hustler.
My delivery packs something heavy
and can be ferocious if necessary.
Lightening motivates me to keep shining.
My vulnerability is like thunder,
It echoes the raw emotions
that are buried inside my heart!

My eyes pour like rain down and
flood the shore of my dark cheeks.
I create waves from the tears I cry out.
After the rain, the sun appears and
I wear my big and bright signature smile.
Life can sometimes knock the wind out of you,
but I now have regained my second wind.

I often like to retreat into a secluded area
to do some of my most intimate writing.
Preferably a nice warm log cabin in the mountains.
I may get a glimpse of the snowfall
that likes to visit during the winter season.
Whenever I'm in the mood for romance,
my hand becomes one with my pen and
there is every freaky intention behind each stroke.

My mind controls my thoughts and actions.
My hands love to play and explore what I could
potentially do with my future lady.
I'm passion personified, my sex drive is amplified,
and I'm a distinguished gentleman.
What I write will make the hairs stand up
on the back of my baby's neck.

I'm not a boogeyman, but I can definitely get my boogie on.
All she gotta do is put her back into it.
I think I'll rock her world like an earthquake.
So, if she wants to rock then that's how we can roll.
My skills have not eroded or plateaued...
they have elevated and become more effective over time.
I know how to take my time, I know how to speed it up,
beat it up, and I know how to switch it up.

Rhythm and timing are necessary
for the right kind of precision I'm aiming for.
Don't get wrapped too much into my foreplay,
because when it's all said and done,
I'll have everything wrapped up nice and tight.
I'll be her beau and she can be my ribbon in the sky
for all time like Stevie Wonder.
The forecast is sunny with clear skies and
we can expect temperatures to rise
in the next few days or possibly even weeks.
Don't sweat it baby,
I'm just writing up a storm
to give us a change of scenery.

Gambler

I have a confession. I was once a gambler.
Once upon a time I would make regular
and frequent trips to the casinos.
They were some of my favorite hangout spots.
I loved it so much that I even got a job working there.
I don't know why I enjoyed working in a place
that carried the stench of cigarettes.
People came in all hours of the day and night
and pretty much had one clear objective,
TO WIN SOME MONEY!! I had the same goal,

and I was determined to win as much as I could.

I had this crazy obsession for playing the slot machines.
I started off playing the pennies,
then I worked up the courage to play the dollar machines.
I donated my money to what I eventually
learned to be a bad habit.
These machines would get fed my hard-earned money
and I was just willing to give it away like nothing.
I had this love-hate with slot machine games I was playing.
I'd win some and lose some, but
I would say I lost more often than I ever won.

I would drive home absolutely heartbroken,
and I would think to myself, how could I be so stupid!
I always thought even if I was down,
I could come back and make up the difference.
I would gain a bit of momentum,
but the slots would toy with me and play me for a fool.
I couldn't blame anyone for my irresponsible behavior.
I was in complete denial.
I always viewed gambling as a fun activity
until it stopped becoming fun for me.

Bills needed to get paid, and
I barely could pay them or
sometimes not pay them at all.
I had a serious addiction.
I exposed myself to an environment
that was the devil's playground.
I lived on the edge. I took my chances.
I thought I had nothing to lose.
Gambling is a self-destructive condition.
I had symptoms of addiction.
I was a victim of my own self afflictions.
If you were to make a prediction,
I would say don't bet on me.

Usually, I'm ultra-confident in my abilities,
but I also understand my limitations as well.
It didn't matter if I was on my game or not.
The casinos were rigged to win every time.
They always made sure they got paid first!
They are designed to set you up for failure.
Take it from someone with real experience,
your best bet is not to become a
degenerate, impulsive gambler.

Trust me when I say it all catches up to you in the end.
Gambling isn't done just in the casino.
Life is full stakes and most of us gamble
with decisions we make each day.
Priorities are thrown out the window
and traded in for high risks and sometimes low reward.

The odds tend to be against you,
but you can always play the hand your dealt with
and try to make something happen.
The question is, what are you willing to lose?
Gambling is not an investment,

it's a money scheme to rob you
of what you hold most precious....
YOUR MONEY!!

People can also gamble with their time.
Time is currency and
time is something you never get back.
Money you can get back,
but time can be taken away from you every day.
Gambling doesn't equate to stewardship.

There can be a reward but is it really worth
spending more than you can potentially get.
And even if you get an amount you're satisfied with,
you must ask yourself is it ever really enough?
Not trying to tell you how to live but
being a gambler can ruin your life.
It can cost you everything.
Is that a price you're willing to pay?
Are you an investor or a gambler?
Choose wisely.

Cheerleader

I remember when I was in high school
I used to watch the cheerleaders perform their routines
on the sidelines of a football game.
They had on the most beautiful uniforms
that showed off our school colors.
Red and white.
They had their pom poms
they always would strut their stuff.

Our cheerleaders were our school's pride and joy.
I would always see them cheer on the athletes and
jocks and thought to myself if only I were one of those guys.
Lol. But I carved out my own path and found my niche.
I ran track and I was involved in
All Student Body Leadership
and not to mention All Student Body Historian.
I always wanted to be cheered on, but
for some reason I didn't get a whole lot of love.

It's all good though.
I know it was highly debated
if cheerleading was an actual sport.
In my eyes, cheerleading has always been a sport
because there was always competition among rival schools
or other schools in the state.
The preparation it takes for cheerleaders
to do what they do amazes me.
It takes focus, balance, coordination, concentration,
repetition, encouragement, teamwork, and a good attitude!

I always found most of the cheerleaders very attractive
and that's still true til this day.
I remember seeing how strong and fit

most cheerleaders were,
but what impressed me the most
were how intelligent they were.

To pull off those routines you have to be pretty sharp.
Cheerleaders are professional performers,
and they got some really good dance moves.
I'm a dancer and I can appreciate the moves
to the music they shake their bodies to.

A cheerleader is more than just someone who cheers a team on.
A cheerleader is someone special who is there for you.
They encourage you to do your best!
A cheerleader is someone
who has your back through thick and thin.
Cheerleaders are there when the storms come
and can stand in the rain with you.
Even on your worst days
your cheerleader will still sing your praises.

I have found myself to be a cheerleader
for many of my closest family and friends.
One day I hope to find a wife to cheer on
and be her cheerleader.
I need my wife to be my cheerleader as well.
I know we'll give each other love and affection.
Together we would make the perfect squad!

There is someone who reminds me of a cheerleader,
and she is someone I enjoy seeing every chance I get.
I cheer for this incredible woman every time she gets up on stage.
Her name is _____.
There are many cheerleaders out there,
but I think she is my #1 choice!

I know I have people rooting for me and
I know she has people rooting for her too.
But I hope we can be on the same team someday
and we can both cheer one another on!
So, with that said, life is too short to be a hater,
so why not be a cheerleader!!
If you're a cheerleader, then
you will find your cheerleader,
I promise you!

This

You don't need to be perfect for this!
You can come as you are to this!
Baby, you know I've been praying for this!
Bet you didn't know I could love you like this!
You need this version of me in your life right now.
I need this version of you in my life too.
This isn't a game.
This is a new beginning.
Together as one we're winning.
It took us a while to get to this point.
This is the best day of my life!

Standing with you at this altar
has been a dream come true.
This moment is something
I've wanted for quite a long time.
I'm sure you wanted this just as bad as I did.
This memory I'll always remember for the rest of my life.
This is a day I'll rejoice because
I finally found what I was searching for...
a precious wife to call my own!
This is what God's plan was all along.
I truly thank God for this!

Trust Issues

I got trust issues, but I'm not the only one.
Most of us have this nagging problem.
I can't speak for anyone else,
but for me it's not like I don't want to trust people.
It's just that I've had some really
bad experiences in the past.
I'm sure some of you have too.
Nowadays, you got people scheming and
trying to get over on other people.

Sometimes, people mistake your kindness for weakness.
They think you're stupid.
Some people talk a good game, and
they try to pull on your heart strings to manipulate you.
I've always seemed to have the most
complications with women.
I know that no one is perfect, but
I've encountered some ladies t
hat have had questionable character
and didn't have my best interest at heart.
There have been guys that were con-men
that screwed me over
and not kept their end of the bargain.
Too many lies and too many red flags
have been shown to me
that I can't really trust most women these days.

I know there are some women
that have had a hard time trusting men too
it goes both ways honestly.
When you've been burned by people

you become a little more guarded and more skeptical.
It's really about just protecting yourself from being hurt.
I can tell you that I'm not the type of person
you want to play with.
Nobody wants to get played and
no one has time to play games.
So, now you know why I have trust issues!
Can you really blame anyone
for having trust issues these days?

Value

There is a word that gets mentioned
almost everywhere you go
or in some kind of public setting.
This word is called value.
So, what exactly is value?

There are a few definitions to describe value.
First, value is the monetary worth of something.
Secondly, value means a fair return or equivalent of
goods, services, or money for something exchange.
Thirdly, value could also mean relative worth,
or importance of good value at the price
most of us usually associate value as a monetary price
or something of worth money is valuable for sure
but it's not the only thing that is valuable in life.

Value is something people put high importance on
or whatever they find useful to them
most people base their entire lives
on something called core values
for example, when I was in the US Air Force
there were some core values we swore by
they were integrity first
service before self
and excellence in all we do.
I have adopted these values
added them to other values I have in my life

What are your values?
I value God health, time, family, friends,
kindness, honesty, loyalty, empathy, appreciation,
and courage, to name a few.
I value these things because I care about them very much

I guess a better way to say it is
I'm very passionate about them
some people value material things
rather than valuing people

I have noticed a lot of people value their pets
more than people nothing wrong with valuing pets
because they are a part of your family.
People have free will to do what they want
or believe what they feel is right or good for them.
It doesn't mean it's always the best-case scenario

God values humanity because he loves us all
if God the creator of Heaven and Earth,
didn't value us we wouldn't cease to even exist
God wants to have a relationship with us
most people desire to have relationship with others too
life is precious and it's something we should value
and not take for granted
you matter because you have value
never forget that!

Toy

Baby, I want to be your toy that you enjoy playing with.
Except, I only have one condition,
you can't get bored with me and play with another toy.
I'm a toy you'll never get tired of.
I'm action-packed, entertaining, valuable, fun, durable,
appealing, pleasurable and easy to hold on to.
Trust me, you'll never want to let go of me.

Kids play with toys all the time,
but somewhere along the line we all grew up and
we were told not to play with toys anymore.
Ridiculous! There's a time to be serious but
there's also a time to be curious and have a little fun.

Toys come in all shapes and sizes.
I'm the kind of toy that will rub you the right way.
I'm built to last baby!
I'm a toy you're meant to love.
I'm a toy that will bring you so much joy.
I'm better than your Barbie or Cabbage Patch dolls.
Hell, even Ken don't got s*** on me!
I'm just saying.

Play with me and see
how I'll play with your emotions.
I'm a toy that is always in motion.
You don't need any batteries
because I'm fully operational!
I could keep going and going and
going like the Energizer Bunny.
Put away that dildo. You don't need it!
You got me and I got you baby.
I know exactly how to vibrate.

But I also know how to make you feel sensations
you never quite felt before.
I know I may sound too good to be true,
but honey believe me I'm satisfaction guaranteed.
I don't require you to spend any money
except if you wanna make it rain.
When you play with me,
the only thing it's going to cost us is some clothes!

I'm a toy that flirts.
I don't even mind if we talk dirty to one another!
And if you wanna get serenaded,
I'll even sing to you baby.
I'm a toy with no limits.
I'm a toy that's going to keep
that same energy every time we meet.

I'm better than Toys R Us,
I think I put them out of business.
I'm the kind of toy your friends want to have.
I can see why, that's why they envy you.
Please feel free to share this Toy Story with anybody.
I don't mind, just remember
I'm the best toy you've ever had and
I'll always be your favorite toy.
Come back and play with me anytime.

You're Not Meant For Everybody

Some things are meant for you,
while others things just simply are not intended for you.
Just like things, people are not meant for everyone,
and everyone isn't meant for you either!
It's a hard truth to accept sometimes.
A bitter pill to swallow for sure.

People come in a variety of flavors.
Some things just don't mix.
Good chemistry is necessary for a great friendship.
It's a recipe for success!
If your chemistry isn't there,
then it's more likely a recipe for disaster!

People can be good or bad for your health.
People can be medicine or
they can be downright toxic!
Most people will take you for face value
and not really understand your true motive.
Sometimes, we think we can make people like us.
Unfortunately, it doesn't work that way.

You could be the coolest person on earth and
there will still be someone that
doesn't like you for whatever reason.
You can change what you do or how you react,
but you can't control what people think, do, or say!
Never forget that!
If you're looking for that special somebody,
just stop and let it come find you.

Pursue your dreams, passions, and goals.
It's not your business what people say or think of you.

You're one of a kind.
There is no one like you and
there has never been anyone like you
or anyone that will be like you
after you're long gone from this place.

Enjoy being you.
Pursue relationships but don't get hung up
if they don't work out like you hoped for.
Don't live in the past. Make new memories.
You're not meant to please everyone.
You're meant to be your own wonderful creation.
You're meant to be loved,
but you're required to give love too.
Even if you're not meant for everybody!

Selfish

I've been told I was selfish one too many times.
To be honest, I was taught to
fend for myself my whole life.
I didn't want to be selfish but on the real I had to be.
If we are really being honest,
we all in some ways are selfish.
I know I'm not the only one.

I believe that self-care is by no means selfish.
If you don't care about yourself then who will?
Sometimes, I can get too caught up in myself
that I lose sight of what's really going on around me.
It's not the way I'm trying to be honestly,
I'm just your normal everyday hustler.

Responsibility is put on your shoulders
and you are left carrying the weight of it.
I want to give and I actually love to give,
but how can you pour from an empty cup?
Sometimes, people can drain you.
Time, money, and energy are resources
that need to be used properly.
They must be protected and preserved at the same time.

Sometimes, self needs help.
When the time comes for you to need some help,
you sometimes find yourself all alone.
Nothing but crickets.
I don't mean to play the violin of my emotions,
but I'm beating on the drum of my truth!
I remember helping people in their time of need
and I was glad to lend them a hand.

But it's nice when someone can return the favor.
I learned that you can help people,
but you got to help yourself first.
When you ride in the airplane and
in the event of an emergency,
you put on your oxygen mask first
before you help anyone else.
At least that's what I would do.
I can't speak for anyone else.
The world was ripened to be selfish.

The bad side to getting selfish is that
people can tend to make it all about them.
It's an ugly trait no doubt about it.
As much of a bad rap selfishness gets,
what people don't get is that selfishness
could be used as a means for survival.
Selfishness could be seen as you play for keeps.

One thing I will say is
that as much as you want to keep,
you'll have to give it all back eventually.
All the things we acquire, we won't be able to
take with us after we are long gone.
Be self-motivated but don't have selfish motives.
Don't make your ministry to be all about "self."
Sometimes you gotta put yourself on the shelf
or be forced to be put on the shelf.
Most things you can do yourself,
but at the end of the day we all need community...
none of us are immune to that aspect.

Getting caught up in yourself is a trap.
Don't fall for it. After pride comes the fall.
Don't get caught slippin' or else you'll fall victim.
Selfishness can be an addiction,

break the habit and stop claiming that you're self-made.
You made a career of being selfish.
It's time to retire from it and
think of something more
other than just yourself!
Aren't you tired of being selfish?

Ignorance

There is a fragrance I smell in the air,
it's not the most appealing scent at all.
Nothing clean, smooth, or cool about it.
I know this all too familiar smell.
It's the stench of ignorance.
I don't have much of a tolerance for it period.
But they say ignorance is bliss.
I just wish people would piss it out of their system.
I get it. We don't know everything there is to know,
but at least try to learn or do some research.
Ignorance is borderline stupidity.
It's a red flag, so don't ignore it!
Ignorance is like a mental illness,
the only cure for it is wisdom.
Time to stop overlooking facts and
seek the truth of the matter.
Take off the blinders and open your eyes.

Ignorance doesn't unlock Pandora's box.
Ignorance is a form of laziness and misinterpretation.
Before its conception, we knew ignorance as bliss.
Some people never pass up any chance to be ignorant.
I would like to bypass it altogether,
but I have to admit that sometimes I'm ignorant too!
I see ignorance sprayed on building walls like graffiti.
Hearts and minds alike are vandalized by ignorance.
Society is ignorant of saying, it is what it is.
Although it may be true,
doesn't mean that is an acceptable explanation.
If you don't know something,
ask the question or just do some research!

Finding Her and Finding Myself

Together means "to get her."
But how can I get her when it
doesn't seem I can get through to her?
There is no way I can force her to be mine.
I don't own her. But make no mistake that I want her.
I want her to realize that I look at her through "real eyes."
The eyes are the portals into the spirit.
She can see into my heart.

My intentions are clear but I fear
she is afraid of my past.
I kind of suspect that she doesn't want
to give me the time of day.
But regardless, I stand before her and
present my best self to appeal to her.
My heart reveals what I've always tried to conceal.
My face surely doesn't lie about how I feel about her.
At the same time, I don't want to get caught up
in my feelings either.
Feelings can be a good indicator
but a horrible tour guide.

I want something that comes naturally
but I need more of the supernatural.
I pray that God makes a way and
I know that He will.
I want her to see me for the man that I am.
I want her to see me beyond the flesh.
I want her to see me better with fresh eyes.
Vision should never be obstructed in any way.
I just want to be in the clear and endear myself too only her.
I look at the man in the mirror every day and
I know I'm a work in progress, but I like who I'm becoming.

The woman I see in front of me can be my mirror and
reflect what I try to show from my actions.
But there is a wall standing between us.
I want to break it down with the strength
of my determination and passion.
No obstacle will deter me from meeting my true desire!
I'm wired for love and I'm willing do what is required.
But it's up to her to choose.

She can have any man she wants.
Or she can choose to go through life alone.
I want to be there, but I won't intrude if she wants her space.
I know my place, so I embraced her from a distance.
In order for me to get her means
that she will have to meet me halfway.
I need her to allow me access into her boundaries but
assure her of constant protection and affection.
She has to feel comfortable enough to trust me with her heart.
She is strong but delicate at the same time.

I have to be very careful with her.
I have to be gentle but also firm when I need to be.
I want to pollinate her like a honeybee
with a cherishing love that will keep her
blooming through all seasons!

Maybe in time she will open up to me.
Or maybe not.
If I don't get her then at least I'll have me.
I can find myself in a special one,
but I can find myself even more
when I discover it within myself.

The Last Laugh poem

When they hear my name, they laugh at me.
When they see me, they like to continue the laughter.
Behind my back the laughs grow even louder.
Like hyenas they become tickled with hysteria.
But it isn't until I roar like a lion
that it makes them pause and get shaken.
I said, they heard me roar and
I had to let them know that I'm no joke.
I'm a king and this is my domain.
I'm at the top of the food chain and I'm a real beast!
The least you subjects can do
is recognize greatness when you see it.

People are often blind with ignorance,
prejudice, envy, and jealousy.
I'm not the one to go at, meet Mr. Aaron Woodson.
I'm a heavyweight and I know my way around the ring.
Run me my respect and roses.
Mockery is foolishness and my stock is all the way up!
Like Fat Joe, yesterday's price isn't today's price!
I'm not having any more disrespect on my name.
Ya'll can laugh now but you'll definitely cry later.
As of now I'm living my best life.
When you're laughing, I'll just keep passing you all by.
If I wanted to, I could pull up and do a drive by...
but I'm not with the violence.
I'd rather silence and humble you instead.
Now, how's that for a last laugh?

The Angel That Watches Over You

I put the past version of myself into a  and
I emerge now as a new and improved spiritual being!
All my fears, worries, and doubts are
somewhere blowing in the wind.
Looking back at my exes like a pillar of salt.
I know my faults but as long as I humble myself before God,
He will exalt me in due time.

All these things been dangling on my heart strings.
The sorrows I sing about my life have been full of the blues.
But don't you ever forget that this guy has got plenty of rhythm!
I drop them hammers like Thor. I'm full of that thunder!
I let them all marvel at my greatness.
I've been a little behind on my delivery, so I got time today.
So, here's the package I'm giving to ya.
I got every reason to be fed up sometimes,
there are times things get way too out of hand.
I almost get out of pocket but
I remember the great sacrifice He made for me.
He knows my heart but He also taught me better than that too.
I know better, so I gotta do better.

I was captive to my sin and He set me free.
The presence of God captivates my soul.
Yes, there are times when my soul gets weary.
My eyes get a little teary,
however, I know that my Father counts every tear
as I must count it all joy.
I rejoice because I know where I'll be someday.
I'll be with Him for an eternity
when He wants to call me home.
But while I'm here I must continue the course of life

and do the work that God has called me to do!
I'm present for now but eventually
I'll be absent from the body and present with the LORD!
Ascend I must, so don't try to clip my wings.
I'll be an angel and remember
the angels keep watching over you!

Nipple

There is something that I find so fascinating, arousing, and
stimulating about seeing a sneak peak of something so beautiful.
The object of affection I speak of is called a nipple.
I know it's a weird obsession.
Nipples especially on a very attractive woman
seem to greet me almost at every turn.
Especially if it's a cold or wet day and
a woman is wearing a white t-shirt or tank top!

Nipples like to stand at attention, and they appear hard as rocks.
I find myself almost being hypnotized by them.
I try not to lust, but I must guard my eyes
to withstand the seductive torment.
Nipples just be looking like missiles and are attached to supple
breasts. Instinctively and primarily, I want to suck on them.
Nipples always seem like they want to escape
or bust out of a bra.
They seem to want to be free.

Nipples need to breathe.
Nipples don't seem very conservative at all.
Nipples are very reactive to the sensation of touch and stimulation.
Nipples come in all shapes and sizes.
Babies are breast-fed by a nipple.
Sometimes, I get a little jealous because
I want to get a taste of a precious nipple.
Nipples are natural, they should not be censored or canceled.
Nipples are ripe and they seem to want attention and be played with.

It's no different than flicking the bean if you know what I mean. *lol*
By no means, am I saying go touch or grab someone's nipple.
But if we are all honest with ourselves,
we have all liked a good nipple in our lifetime!

256

There are times we must conceal the nipple,
because if we don't people may get offended
if you have a wardrobe malfunction.

Think Nipple Gate at The Superbowl
(Janet Jackson & Justin Timberlake).
Nipples serve a purpose; life is hard enough already.
There is nothing wrong with enjoying nipples.
Don't discriminate against them.
Show nipples some love!

I'm not ashamed to say that I love nipples.
I am biologically wired to like them.
So, if you see a nipple that pops into your view, just carry on!
It's not the end of the world.
Nipples existed a long time ago and
they'll be around long after you're gone!
Long live the nipple!

Goin' Off

Let me get off my ass because I'm about to start goin' off up in here!
I'm born ready, like Fugees Ready or Not Here I Come.
My poetry hits hard like a drum. Have you going dumb.
These rhymes leavin you shook and leavin' you numb.
Percussion causing you to have concussions.
I hit em up style better known as my crazy style.
You know how I be wildin'!
Come through in the building like a gorilla.

I set it off in the spot.
I ain't afraid to say it with my chest that I'm the best!
All the hate and stress need to be laid to rest.
I ain't with that mess.
I'm back in my bag of tricks, I'm real slick with it.
Ya'll just stay sick wit it!

Had to tap into my big energy and bring out the monster!
I had a lay off until I decided to pop off again!
Like Mase, I came back to fly lids off!
I ain't taking no more days off.
Watch me bring the heat. I'm the original sizzler!
Stupidity and entitlement turn me off,
intelligence and gratitude are the new flex.

People slack off,
always running to go here and there.
Just be everywhere!
Certain thrills can get most of us off...
I'm ready to break my shorty off!
We run a few plays and get off to a great start and finish!!
I am playing for keeps. I love when she sleeps
and before she wakes up, it will be much deeper than that!
We just can't stay off each other.

We got some serious fire and desire going on up in here.
We shootin' off like fireworks on 4th of July!
It's a celebration! I've always knew how to tee off!
But one thing I don't have to worry about
is her missing outon pleasures she likes!

Sometimes I just want to show off.
She always makes sure she taps in.
I always try to make her sound off and tap out!
I ain't UFC but my ground game is vicious.
My hard work pays off. I got skills to pay the bills.
My stock is going up. My momentum can't drop off.

I'm taking off to greater heights.
Got dreams in my sights. No time to get lost, I will find my way.
My door of opportunity is right around the corner.
I'm riding this thing until the wheels fall off!
Take your hats off for a real one.
I'm a champion and there ain't nothing stoppin' me.
You better believe I'm going off!

Chip on your Shoulder

You ever have something that just rubbed you the wrong way?
Like you have this big chip on your shoulder!
People be like are you mad?
Why you mad?
Why you acting like that?
There is a reason why I got this chip on my shoulder,
I didn't put it there!
People think they can say or do anything
and act like it's all good.
People smiling all up in your face
knowing damn well they don't like you.
Pretending to be down with you
when they secretly plotting to get one over on you!
Fake love coming from all these snakes.
I have the authority to trample over scorpions and serpents.
They lucky I don't step on any of them!

Even the ones closest to you can do the most damage.
They've been supportive and
loyal all the way up until now.
They see you grow and the gap has widened
between you and them.
You are on your path and they are still in the same place.
Little did you know that they were jealous of you all this time.
Those same people who claimed they loved you or
had love for you just stabbed you in the back.
Damn, that just ain't right!

Everyday it's a fight to stay calm and take the high road!
When the chips are down and believe me,
those chips will come down at some point in your life...
you'll begin to see whose really got your back!
Sometimes we are on a job that overworks and under pays us!!

We get no appreciation or recognition for
how much we bust our ass!
You expect me to do more with less.
You expect me to have a positive attitude and
you treat me with so much disrespect.
You got to be kidding me!
And all these people out here playing games
in the dating world is just wild to me!
Can't get straight answers anymore.
There is a lack of substance, character, communication,
and most importantly respect!

When I speak my frustrations, you think I'm just complaining or
blowing things out of proportion!
Excuse me, why don't you put your selfish ass in my shoes and
see how you feel if someone did the same shit to you.
You should know better.
But I'm not gonna hold a grudge.
I'm gonna drop this Boulder and
relieve myself from carrying a heavy load.
I have a responsibility and
I don't have to carry a chip on my shoulder for nothing!
Don't let a chip on your shoulder wear you down,
it's not worth it!

Russian Roulette

Russian Roulette is a lethal game of violence and
can spell doom for anyone that dares to play or
becomes a victim of circumstance.

Russian Roulette involves a gun,
particularly a revolver loaded with one single round.
There is a possibility someone can be killed by one single shot.
Most people in life are playing Russian Roulette.

What's your bullet?
Like seriously, what's going to be the bullet that takes you out?
You may be fortunate to escape without any serious injury.
Notice I didn't mention death because
at some point eventually with all have a date with our fate.
There's no fighting it at all!

However, there are some things that can shorten our lifespans.
For example, you have drug and alcohol abuse,
tragic accidents, abuse of prescription drugs,
being poisoned, stress, death penalty, etc.

Anything can happen to anyone at any given time.
Life already has enough ammunition to cause your demise,
don't give it anymore ammo!
Life doesn't play,
stop treating it like Russian Roulette!

The Ladder

An invention that comes to mind that helps with
ascension and descension is better known as a ladder.
Ladders are tall and can extend a good measurable distance.
A ladder is useful for places that are difficult to reach.
A ladder wouldn't be a ladder without steps.
Each step you take matters.

We climb the ladder for a purpose as it can provide
stability, direction, and strength in our lives.
Ladders are reliable and helpful when they need to be,
but they are kind of like a lifeline.
They can save your life ladies and gentlemen.
If you don't believe me, ask your local firefighters!

Ladders can primarily be seen on fire trucks around the city.
Ladders make a firefighter's job a whole lot easier.
Ladders can make or break your fall.
Being around a ladder is great for safety.

In fact, it's necessary!
People every day may climb a real-life ladder
or could experience a ladder visiting their dreams.
Ladders are meant for assistance.
In Corporate America, employees climb the
"Corporate Ladder" to make a promotion.

A ladder can represent hierarchy, but
it encourages us to take steps; to keep going.
Even when people try to knock you off the ladder, you're on.
Even if you're afraid of heights!
A ladder gives us a leg to stand on so to speak!
Ladders get stepped on,
but they are not abused whatsoever!

You're not a doormat
but be a ladder to someone.
People need you!
You could be the very ladder
that saves their life.

We Gotta Do Better Black Men

Dear Black Men,
Like Pac, all eyes are on us!!
I am writing to let you know that no matter what,
someone will always be watching us.
Whether it be other races or faces,
family, friends, enemies, children, women, and men.
The pressure mounts our shoulders, but
as kings we can carry the burden that others never knew existed.
WE EXIST... we are out here!
They see us and they know we are kings!
It's time that we acknowledge that fact ourselves and
that people get put on notice! We are not trash.
We are not troublemakers.
We are not lazy or good for nothing.
We are not niggaz!

We need to live up to our name and birthright!
We don't need to sag our pants to show off our behinds.
Let's wear the belt of truth fellas
along with wearing the armor of God!
We need to show off the leaders that we naturally are.
We are looked upon to lead.
We are chosen to be difference makers!
People count on us to do the right thing.
We have the power to affect real change.
We are change agents and we are
weapons of mass enlightenment.
We may have skin that is dark as night,
but we are called to be the light.
It's time for us to take flight, Black Men!

It's time for us to SOAR!
It's time for us to ROAR like the mighty lion.
We have dominion, we are not the world's minions.
We are wealthy in mind, heart, body, and soul.
We have the capability to make huge financial gains
because we have that strong entrepreneurial spirit.
We have a work ethic that is tougher than shoe leather.
We are the polish that shines for everyone to see!
People are fascinated by us.
We carry magic that is powerful.
We will live on generational curses, but
we can break them by giving
God full control over our lives.

Sometimes, we receive unfair criticism and
sometimes people will sing our praises.
That's what comes with the territory of being a black man.
We can't afford to be ignorant of the enemies' tactics.
Like Denzel said, "At your highest moment,
be careful, the devil comes for you!"
We can't slap our way into greatness.
We can't achieve success by acting a fool.
It's time for us to call out the King in ourselves and
live up to the kingship we are called into.
Black Men, they are not going to give us a pass
for reacting to disrespect or misconduct.

We have to learn how to exercise restraint and
remember that God is our defender.
We don't have anything to prove to anyone.
Black Men we need accountability, and
we need to reject passivity.
We also need to be courageous and be intentional!
Black Men, we know there are systems designed
to slow us down, discourage us, hurt us,
imprison us and discredit us!

We are powerful and can overcome
anything that comes our way.
We are not meant to be oppressed.
We are not meant to lack anything.
We are not meant for mediocrity.

We are not meant to abuse and be abused.
We are meant for greater.
Please, understand the assignment!
We are built to be Kingdom Men and nothing less.
Black Men, I know we don't always get the love, accolades,
and respect that we so rightfully deserve...
but understand that you are loved, appreciated,
needed, wanted, respected, and recognized.
If not in this life, then the next!
We can't make any excuses. Nobody cares.
We must find a way to get it done no matter what.
Black Men you don't have to act hard
when you're already as hard as diamonds!
I see you striving out here Black Men,
I'm striving along with you, my brothers.
As my band of brothers,
we just gotta do better Black Men!!

Failure

I've failed countless times.
It's very discouraging knowing you give it your all
and you just can't seem to get it right.
I worked so hard to try to overcome
the adversity I was up against.
I've had my share of successes in the past,
but failure always hovered around me like a dark cloud.
It's hard to be proud of yourself when
all it seems like you ever do is lose!
Every day I wake up is a win.
But as we all know life is quite fleeting and
eventually, we all lose our lives.

I've lost money, jobs, friends, relationships, opportunities,
cars, and valuables one too many times.
The worst thing I've learned to lose is myself.
I've lost patience. I've lost hope.
I've even lost my temper on some occasions.
All because of the agony of frustration.
I know we are not supposed to be defined by our failures, but
it seems the world labels us by them.
On the other side of success, there is failure.
They are two sides of the same coin.
I failed people, I failed my country,
I failed my family, I failed myself,
and I failed God.

I failed miserably and with tears in my eyes,
it looks like I have nothing to show
for what I've done or tried to do.
I wanted to deliver better results,
but I came up really short.
I failed to start my own family.

I failed not having a wife.
I failed not getting a chance to be a husband.
I failed academic classes.
I failed to stay in shape.
I failed to own a home.

Failure is the manure of growth.
It's not that I don't try to learn
from my failures and mistakes,
but sometimes things just don't work out no matter
how well planned or prepared you are.
Hey, nobody's perfect.
The best thing about failure is at least you can keep trying.
Repeated failures hurt and they suck!
No one plans to fail.
But you certainly fail when you fail to plan.

Failure is devastating.
It's an indescribable pain you feel that just nags at you!
There are no guarantees in this life.
You're not owed success.
Failures mean you are paying
your dues to invest in your success.
We are not OUR failures...
failures are just trial and error!
Eventually, we'll all get it right at some point.
Remember, there is absolutely no way
you can avoid the lessons of failure!
Keep failing, you're much closer to success than you think.
Keep going, keep growing, keep failing!!!

Success

Success comes dressed up in many different outfits.
It's not one size fits all.
Success requires a different version outside of your normal self.
A lot of people want success but
they don't want to put in the work or pay the cost.
If you think Success should be handed to you
then you've already lost the game.
You're not entitled to be successful.

To know success, you must become familiar with failure.
To know success, you must know sacrifice.
Success looks different in the eyes of various people.
Success can look like a stranger you haven't been introduced to.
It can be foreign to most people that haven't tasted it before.
It can even be a dangerous endeavor to embark upon at times.
There is no problem having success but
sustaining that success can be problematic.
Success is never automatic, there are no guarantees.
Success will find you when you're traveling
on the path to your purpose.

To be successful, you must be intentional.
Before you receive success,
you must believe you are already successful.
But you also must prepare yourself for success.
Most people don't plan to fail, but they fail to plan.
Most of us I'm sure would like to get things right the first time.
Failures and mistakes give you
the opportunity to learn and grow.
Understand that you can't be successful all by yourself,
more than likely you had some help along the way.
When you become successful,
remember to have an attitude of gratitude.

Appreciate the people who helped
or invested in your success.
Oh, and don't forget my friend, success has enemies.
Jealousy is a bitter adversary of success.
It roots against your achievements and
wants to see you down and defeated.
Let me remind you that if you're born of God,
you're born to win.

Success is a gift worth holding onto,
don't squander it or do anything foolish.
Success is my personal recommendation for anyone to have.
When you know that it means
you know that you have a sense of worth.
Success is worth celebrating with people you love.
Remember, not everybody loves you or your success. Period.
Overcoming obstacles and challenges build character.

Success can come with 😊 buzz or it can be silent.
It can also be a surprise to where it freaks a lot of people out.
You deserve success,
just treat yourself like a king or queen!
Success is yours for the taking!!!

The Enforcer

Close your beaks when a real one speaks!
Let me break it down for you.
See, I ain't even reached my peak yet!
Watch me strut like a peacock...
you can't ruffle these feathers.
I'm spreading these wings and getting ready to take off.

Lay off the hate, don't you know its toxic...
it's not good for you silly rabbit!
Hatin' is a bad habit, you need to kick it to the curb,
or you might just kiss the curb!
Success is my favorite kind of herb...
I like to stay lit; haters don't want this smoke.
I'm not the butt of your corny jokes...
choke on your words.
Now who gets the last laugh.

You can't handle this spice,
better think twice when you try to pull up.
I grew up on the block...
I stay armed and ready.
Don't make me use your weak ammunition against you...
mark my words I'm a lethal weapon.
I shoot straight at you,
like G-Eazy it ain't safe...
it ain't safe!
Better pipe down cuz you are disturbing the peace.
You pushed it to the limit...
best believe I'm a No Limit soldier!

Jumping Through Hoops

If you live long enough, you'll know that you're gonna have to
clear some hurdles and even jump through a few hoops!
You're expected to perform numerous acrobats and stunts,
while juggling your own personal life.
You already got enough clowns in your circus but
on top of that they got you out here looking like a chimpanzee.
Got no time to play games like Yahtzee.
You can play the cards you've been dealt and
try to come out with the upper hand.
I can't stand jumping through a bunch of hoops
to be completely honest with you.
Sometimes it can be frustrating.
It can be exhausting.
It can be ridiculous.
But one part of me says I got this
so go ahead and bring it on!
If they tell me to jump, I'll say "How High!"

However, don't get it twisted.
I'm telling you right now, "don't play with me."
I'm not someone who is going to entertain you
and all your little minions.
I got my dignity, and I will for sure have my respect.
Sometimes when you're planning some sort of event,
you have to jump through a few hoops
to make an occasion a good or memorable one!
Jumping through hoops has its advantages too.
It can be beneficial in receiving certain incentives
and bringing up your morale.
Jumping through hoops builds character
and shows you how to take initiative!
It's an exercise that will keep you on your toes!
So, if you must, keep jumping through those hoops to reach success!

We Ain't Scared

They see us, but they fear us. They can't stand to be near us.
When we speak up, they don't really try to hear us.
Yet they always find a way to try us.
Let me tell you something.
We are not the ones and we got time today!
We're not what you think we are!
Don't underestimate us! We are smarter than you think.
Like chess we gotta stay a few moves ahead of ya.
You got the privilege, but we've got the power.
Stop being sour over us having our finest hour!
We are trying to be celebrated not tolerated.
If we aren't going to be celebrated,
then we will just throw our own party.
We don't need no affiliation to any political party...
we just represent The Black Lives Matter Movement.

Not trying to single anyone out, but all lives need to be protected
especially Black Lives at all costs!!
There seems to be a target on our heads.
Most of us just want to live in peace and harmony, but
somehow you keep disturbing our peace.
You wanna lock us up. You wanna beat us. You wanna lie on us.
You wanna make trouble for us!
You always want to blame it on us.
We breathe the same oxygen as you do, but
you don't really want us here.
Just ask George Floyd.
Oh, that's right, you took his life without any remorse.
You just wanna try to take us out.
You want to erase us from the history books.
And you also want to steal from us!
You want to disenfranchise us.
You want to humiliate us. You don't want us to have anything!

You don't own us. We are not your slaves.
We are not your servants.
We are not second-class citizens.
We are a civilized people.
We are brilliant people. We are a resilient people!!
We not trying to be in a war with you but don't push us.
We are already on the brink.
You might want to rethink your strategy.
We are dangerous minded people that won't take your shit!
There is no quit in us...like Maya Angelou we will rise...
we shall continue to rise!
You shall hear our cries for freedom and
justice like the toll of the Liberty Bell!
We will March to victory and
be your worst nightmare.
We ain't scared!

Too Pretty

If looks could kill. Girl, I'd say you're killin' the game.
Not too sure if I could say the same for anyone else.
You're too pretty for your own good.
You're a gift to this world that God blessed men like me to see.
Your kind of pretty is rare and exotic.
Many men have fallen under the spell of your pretty tricks.
They are hypnotized and mesmerized
by your beautiful deception.

You have had your way on plenty of occasions.
You have used your prettiness to your advantage
to get whatever you desire.
Being a pretty young woman has done you a lot of favors.
You have a history of being pretty.
You always had a pretty bright future.
Not many people have resisted and told you "No."
From the looks of it, not many people
have ever put you in your place.
When you go out with your girls,
most of ya'll think you're too "pretty" to pay for anything.

You enjoy pretty good service because it came with privilege.
If you ask me, pretty is a trap.
You get caught up and the pretty young woman
just has her way with you.
Most women love to flex how pretty they are.
It's like they must prove a point and say that just because
they are pretty then they must be better than you.
They love to wear their pretty long hair or
wear their short hairdos to show off
for various people and social media.
They love to go to the nail salon and
make their nails all nice and pretty.

While they're at it they might as well get a pedicure.
When they get done, they are ten toes down
and get their pretty walk going.
Nothing wrong with being pretty at all
but there has to be more than what's on the surface!
Pretty doesn't impress me. Deep down, pretty is a good cover up.
It's like make-up that hides blemishes or flaws.
Some women I've met have happened to be pretty cool.
And there are some that are pretty but
at the same time can be very foolish!

Some pretty women can do some pretty dumb things
every now and then.
Pretty women can be sweet, appealing, and
revealing all at the same time.
A lot of pretty women I know have gone through a lot in their lives.
Some of them have been hurt and abused.
Some of them have been cheated on, lied on,
and disrespected for no reason.
Pretty women can be depressed which is really sad to me.
Pretty women should be happy and
be able to show off those pretty smiles!
Some pretty women are pretty good in bed
and others are pretty lousy.

Pretty women are sexy as they want to be.
They can draw men to them like bees to honey.
Most pretty women are intelligent and elegant.
Their scent often drives men like me pretty wild.
I love my pretty woman to have pretty lips.
I'm a pretty good kisser and she better be too!
If a pretty woman wants a chance with me
then she better be pretty open!
I want to gaze into her pretty eyes
and see a future between us.

Some pretty women can be
very picky and too judgmental.
They can also be pretty insecure too!

I like my pretty women to have a pretty round-round!
I enjoy pretty women with pretty nice sized chests.
But what makes the difference to me is
if she has a pretty big heart.
I'm excited to meet my pretty woman and
I hope she is pretty excited to see me too!
No woman is too pretty for me even if they think they are...
I like a pretty woman who is pretty confident
and secure within themselves.
Pretty ladies use their pretty good features for entitlement.

Sometimes they find themselves in entanglements
they can't seem to shake off!
Pretty comes with benefits and rewards.
Being pretty doesn't mean you get be a snob to other people!
Pretty is a privilege!
Most women use the fact that they're too pretty to work!
That they are too pretty to be around certain people.
They often claim to be pretty good judges of character.
Sometimes pretty women can be pretty blind.

Good men are invisible to some of you ladies.
Yet your eyes are wide open for the bad boy!
I've noticed some pretty women can be very shallow.
Some pretty women can cook pretty well,
while others not so much.
Some pretty women can be pretty funny.
Some have really good jokes that can make me laugh.
In their pretty little world,
they can often think they can do no wrong.

Don't be a pretty woman having a pity party.

Call your family, a friend, or talk to someone
about your pretty struggles.
Like MJ, you are a P.Y.T.
If I get to have a wife, she will have a
pretty awesome man in her life.
Me and my pretty wife will share
some pretty great memories together!
We'll both be pretty savage and we'll be on top...
at least one of us anyway. Lol.
We'll have pretty good chemistry
that will rock each other's world!
My queen can be pretty as she desires to be.

I know it will cost me a pretty penny
to keep someone like her though.
Pretty women don't come cheap!
Fellas don't ever let a pretty woman intimidate you.
You're pretty good enough to be in her league.
Step up to the plate. Pitch your game.
Show her what you're made of. Show off your skills.
If she doesn't accept you, move on.
There is plenty of pretty fishes in the sea!
Women embrace your pretty self.
Don't be ashamed to be pretty.

Be proud and be confident in yourself!
Pretty comes naturally.
Don't make pretty so cosmetic.
Be authentic like a baseball card.
If pretty women were in the Major Leagues,
it would be a pretty good bet that
some of them would make my All-Star team.
I'd mentor and coach them to
reach a pretty high standard of excellence.
Sounds like a pretty good deal to me!

Their faces of expression are too pretty...
I just want to frame them on my wall of fame.
But only one pretty face with a pretty heart
can be my one and only MVP!
Whoever she is and wherever she is,
remember to stay pretty but
don't disguise it with vanity.
Your spirit must be pretty too!

Left Overs

Stop giving do-overs to people
who treat you like leftovers.
You are a fine cuisine, not chopped liver.
Better yet she thinks she can put you on ice
and thaw you out later.
Nah sis, it doesn't work like that.
She can't even cook anyway,
but she wanna serve you some old leftovers.
What kind of shit is that?
Ladies, stop giving these lame guys your good-good
if they are coming at you with Ramen Noodle game!
He wants you to get a makeover but
he's giving you nothing but leftovers.
There's dudes ain't even got a job and
darn sure can't give you a home.

Yet, you keep accepting this unacceptable behavior
and wonder why he's screwing you over.
Quit giving these jokers do-overs and tell them it's game over!
I know it sucks to let them go, but let it blow over.
You'll be alright. Things will get poppin' again, trust me.
Pretty soon you won't be settling for just scraps,
you'll get everything you deserve and more.
Keep ya heads up you all are a blessing.
You won't be going left because
you'll move in the direction of what's right for you!
Remember, you're Nobody's Leftovers!!

Sh*t End of the Stick

Have you found yourself on the wrong end of the stick
a few times in your life?
I know I have plenty of times.
I once heard it put like this,
we all go through s*** but don't let the s*** get on you!
You're not responsible for everyone else's crap, just yours!
As we all know life isn't very fair now, is it?

Bad things happen.
Whether you're a good or bad person,
no one is exempt.
We might feel some type of way about it,
but it's something we all have to learn to deal with.
Sometimes getting the shit end of the stick
means you not always getting your way.
You don't always get what you want.
That's just the way the cookie crumbles!
Embrace that shit!

Life comes with many disappointments,
trials, hardships, and bullshit.
It comes as no surprise,
shit no matter what is still going to be a piece of shit!
But I got some good news for you,
shit makes things grow.
You have to go through it, so you can grow.
We all know that at any moment that shit can hit the fan,
just remember that it shall pass.
It's a fart..it don't smell good and
it's not a very pleasant odor at all.
Let shit go forgive shit of its trespasses
because it just comes and goes.

If anything, don't try to have a shitty outlook on things. Shit ain't all bad. Tell yourself that you're the shit and you'll come out on the better end of all that other shit! Be grateful you got the shit end of the stick because that shit doesn't stand a chance against you!

The Dog in Me

Some men look at ladies like a whole snack!
But some of ya'll ladies will take a bite of us
like we did a whole crime like McGruff "The Crime Dog."
It's like we're guilty of attraction or something.
I don't know.
Don't act like ya'll don't look at some men
like snacks either, c'mon now!
Don't get all Rottweiler or Pit Bull on us now.
We ain't even had a chance to bury our bone yet.
Calm down! Keep your bad attitude on a leash. Beware of it!
I know your senses detect potential threats but
understand not every man is a threat to you.
I apologize in advance for any man
that has dogged you out in the past.
But it's not cool to dog men out either!
It's really uncalled for to be honest with you!
It's no secret we are attracted to you in the first place.
I don't see any problem with that.

However, I understand the need for
boundaries, respect, and safety.
Excuse me, if you feel we invading your space, but
we all share time and space, right?
All we got is space and opportunity.
Most people go to the pound or
pet store to find a dog they can give a home to.
Some guys are trying to find a home.
They just want a safe place.
Stop jerkin our chain when all we want
to do is keep you company.
But not every dog is wanted.
Some dogs come with fleas.
Some have been on the streets.

Other dogs are just too much to handle.
I guess that's the way some of ya'll feel about us.
I think it can really go both ways honestly.
I just want to be honest and say I'm looking for a loyal partner,
not someone who will kick me like a dog every chance they get.
Sometimes, I'll grrrr...
don't think I'll bite though
it's just my way of speaking to you!
That's just the dog in me!

Best I Ever had

No one will love you more than me and no one ever will.
I held you down for so long, but I realized I had to let you go.
I always believed if you love someone,
you let them go and
if they return, they were meant to be and
if not then it wasn't meant to be.

God knows how much I loved you.
I never wanted to give you up.
That shit was one of the hardest things for me to ever do!
I just wanted to do the right thing.
I wanted you to be happy.
Years have come and gone and
yet you remain in my heart.
I moved on but the residue of you never left me.
It's like I'm haunted by the past and what could have been.
I surrendered myself to God and
He took my cares I placed upon Him.
There is no void but there is a reminder in my life
that tells me I miss you sometimes.

I'm not even gonna lie,
I didn't want to see you with another man.
However, I knew it was for the best for us.
I didn't own you.
And you didn't own me.
We were on borrowed time...
we had our season,
even though it was short but bittersweet.
I don't consider our ending a defeat.
It was only the beginning
of a new chapter for us individually.
I got closure but there were times

I struggled with keeping my composure.

Its 2020 and now I've got clarity
despite all the chaos going on around me in this world.
I believe you still think of me and
its ok if you choose to forget me.
I have no regrets, just lessons in this game of love!
I thank you for being one of the best parts of my life.
I sincerely wish you nothing but the best.
Even though the best is yet to come,
I still think you're the best I ever had.

Free Agent

I'm a free agent, not a special agent.
I must inform you that I represent myself
as single and I'm always ready to mingle!
I haven't been drafted yet,
but I know one day my number will be called!

Most of these ladies recruit the wrong kind of men.
They pick from a class who they think are high value, but
it turns out they are nothing more than total busts!
I've always considered myself
a worthy candidate for selection.
But not all the greats make it to the hall of fame.
Like Deion, I'm prime time!
I'm a highlight waiting to happen! I'm special!
I should be first ballot all the way.
I've always been a contender and never a pretender!
Excuse my ego, it's hard to let it go.

Being passed on is nothing new to me.
I relish my role as an underdog.
I'll continue to fly under the radar and play my position.
I'll wait for my opportunity and
be grateful that I'm still an eligible bachelor.
I have an abundance mindset and
I'm confident I'll find a home that welcomes me.
I'm a prized free agent
to a special woman that decides
I'm her #1 choice!

We Want Justice

Hatred is a disease that is quite common like
a cold there have always been symptoms of it!
Love is the only vaccine to treat its terrible condition.
A soft answer turns away wrath.
Bathing in hate is not good hygiene.
Be pure and kind with your intentions.
Hate went from being footsteps in the dark
to now stepping out of its own shadow!

I told you in my first book, to recognize the face.
This world wears hate as its FACE OF EXPRESSION!
Be of good cheer...we will overcome the world
just like Jesus did before us.
I implore us to rethink our strategies.
This is chess not checkers.
Every action is a reaction which becomes a chain reaction.
Hate is never satisfied...its appetite for destruction
is always needed for its untamed hunger.
What you feed will lead..

I know we have been malnourished of
compassion, understanding, and empathy.
We are not asking for sympathy...
People of color just want to be seen, heard, felt, and to matter!
Our needs can no longer go ignored.
Our pleas for help need to be recognized as a sounding alarm!
Especially when you see a cop putting his knee
on a black man's neck!
I think it's time we put our foot on this country's neck
and reshuffle this deck of cards.

We not playing the race card.

We are just playing the cards we've been dealt with.
Too many jokers wanna play this dangerous game with murder.
Our Kings are dying...our Queens are crying!
We need to respond with the few Aces we have up our sleeves!
Our retaliation will be a ROYAL FLUSH!

Vengeance is mine saith the LORD.
We are at war with the system and against all odds
we will do what is necessary.
Racism, our longtime adversary needs to be defeated!
We will overcome and be victorious
over hate crimes, prejudice, ignorance, oppression,
dysfunction, and injustice once and for all!
WE WANT JUSTICE!!!

Men Like Me

You think I'm all about the chase.
But I'm just trying to stand my ground and
show you what a man is really about.
You have many guys of your choosing to pick from.
But choose wisely.
Not every guy wants you just for your cookie.
Like, Lauryn Hill, there are some guys that are about that thing.
Stop making rookie mistakes and see that man for who he really is.
See me for who I truly am. You rate me on a flawed scale.
I know I'm flawed but you are just as flawed as me.
It's ok if you don't find me attractive but
to think I'm a creep because I find you attractive is quite absurd!
It's not like I'm mind f***ing you or anything!
I have many other things on my mind besides you.

I appreciate how great and appealing you are.
I just wish you could say the same about me!
At this moment, we happen to share the same space.
But I do know my place and I know how to keep my distance.
You say anything to keep a barrier between us.
How dare you choose someone else over me?
You can do that, but I wouldn't recommend it though.
Not to sound like a hater, but he ain't got it like me.

Open your eyes!
I made my own moves and I'm always shaking things up!
I got the heart of a lion. You've seen my credentials.
I signed these checks with my own initials.
You say you're about that residual income.
But I really believe you are on residual B.S.
Cuz it seems like you want more of it...more or less!
You don't owe me nothing, but keep in mind that your attitude
will cost you a few good men. Men Like Me!

Choose Your Hat

I wear many different hats.
Let me go ahead and state these facts.
I'm a young black brotha caught up in this system like so many others.
By no means am I saying I'm a victim,
just a product of my environment.
I know where I come from. I came out of my mother's womb.
Her, my father, and grandparents raised me
to take my place as a young black King!
This isn't a race thing; this is the real thing.

When you see me, you better recognize I'm royalty.
I come from the righteous lineage...the King of all Kings!
I step into His courts with high praise.
He is greater in me than anything in this world!
The enemy knows the greatness that God has placed upon me...
He knows his power is no match for the unstoppable
and mighty will of God!
I stand for something, but at the same time
I find myself having to kneel and remain in a humble posture.

Life sometimes feels like torture but
wait this is nothing compared to what hell is like.
Whatever we loose on earth will be loosed in heaven.
And whatever we bind on earth, will be bound in heaven.
Oh, take me to that wonderful and majestic place O LORD!
Prayer and praise are my weapons,
I must use them not only for my advantage but for His glory.
I don't think you understand...He wrote my story
and knows every detail about me.
He knows the plans for my life, and
He has given me a hope and a future.

I'm full of hope and I am happy
to give the love I have inside of me.
I'm a man, but also a spirit man.
I'm made to do good work.
I'm a son, a brother, nephew, grandson, cousin,
a friend, a co-worker, a student, a husband,
a father, an author, a veteran, a believer,
an overcomer, and so much more!

But my God is everything.
I wear many hats, but God's Holy Spirit
is the best Hat I have ever worn!
Jesus looks good on me any day of the week!
Try him out and He will look
just as good on you as He does on me!
Let us always wear
His love, mercy, and amazing grace!
Choose your hat.

Mud

Welcome to Mudville where water meets dirt,
it's a match made in heaven!
It's been said oil and water don't mix, but
that doesn't seem to be the case with oil and dirt.
It's a collaboration between the two that makes
something special we all love to call MUD!
Its dirty and most of the time people want to avoid it at all costs.
But there are others who love playing in the mud.
There is like this weird attraction they have to it or something.
If you have a truck that has four-wheel drive, then
it makes sense to go out in the mud to do some four-wheeling!
Most people from the country are about that life.
City folk tend to do things not associated with mud.

Some animals love the mud!
Pigs for example love being covered in mud
because it cools them off from the hot temperatures outside.
Mud is like their sunscreen, and
it ensures them protection from the hot sun!
I've even found myself playing in the mud before too.

I played something called Mud Volleyball.
I remember slippin' and sliding all over the court
trying to make a play on the ball.
I look like I was covered in Hershey chocolate.
Oh, I wish, but I was just covered in good 'ol mud!

I ain't gonna lie, it was actually kind of fun!
I hope that my future lady won't mind getting down
and dirty with me every now and then.
Those would be quite interesting encounters indeed!
Even seeing a mud wrestling event with two attractive women
would be something I could envision to be very appealing.
As a soldier I've gone through the mud many times over!

In the field, mud sort of became my best friend!
Mud always found a way to stick close to me like a brother!
It never ever wanted to go away!

Mud can be annoying sometimes
where it can cause these things known as mudslides.
It can give a house serious problem especially
when the house is moved off its foundation!
Mud can mess up the terrain and
cause problems for anyone trying to hike or
walk-through certain territories.
Mud won't hurt you, but it can be a nuisance.
Unless you enjoy wearing those mud facial masks.
Memo to all ladies!
Mud tends to stick around for a while.
So, while you wait remember
don't be such a stick in the mud!

Disassociation

You wanna disassociate from me,
but only wanna reconnect
when you want something from me.
Some of ya'll already told me
see ya later a long time ago.
No worries, ain't no love lost.
I'm still a boss and I keep bossin' up!
You thought you would leave me stuck,
but now I'm stuck up!
I was too busy catching these blessings
while you were over there catching hell.

Oh, don't think for one second
you weren't about to get these flames.
It's a shame how you did me though...
but it's cool I'm happy to
finally extinguish you out of my life.
All you left me with was charred memories.
I always thought you would smoke one with me, but
instead I had to give you all my smoke.

Don't choke up now...
I know it hurts just thinking about it.
Many days and nights I looked out the window
and felt this windowpane.
I feel amazing knowing I have better days ahead of me.
Looks like your best days are behind you.
You lost a good one,
maybe you'll know better next time.
Signing off for the last time.
I'm done with you!

I Played the Games

Growing up as a young thunder cat,
I was pretty Gung-HOOOO...about playing Nintendo.
I'm an 80's baby
that when I was first introduced to the original Nintendo system.
That console was a lot of fun to play.
I was all about Super Mario Brothers of any kind.
And of course, I can't leave out Mike Tyson
Punchout or Duckhunt.
I didn't know the slightest bit about
how many bits a Nintendo system had.
All I knew was that it was a hit.

Today, it would probably be better known
as a smash once it upgraded to a Nintendo Wii.
Sometime after the Nintendo,
I became enamored and obsessed with
the Sega Genesis 16-bit system.
I spent countless hours playing classic games like
Sonic The Hedgehog 1, 2, & 3, Golden Axe,
and Mortal Kombat 1 and 2.
Me and my childhood friends always had
Mortal Kombat tournament marathons against each other!
They were epic and brutal!
No violence ever ensued but
it was very much a competitive battle!

I believe playing Sega was a fun hobby for kids like us!
It certainly kept us out of trouble and in our minds,
we thought we were being productive and having fun!
Then I skipped a few home consoles
to get my very first Sony PlayStation.

297

It was the first next generation home console that
used a disc instead of a cartridge.
The graphics were so much more
improved compared to its predecessors.
I remember playing games like
God of War, Street Fighter Alpha, and Mortal Kombat Trilogy.
I thought I was a badass playing these games once mastered them.

My favorite system came not too long after and
it was the Sony PlayStation 2.
This system was significantly better than
the original Sony PlayStation.
There was a huge game library accessible much
to the delight of gamers everywhere.
I enjoyed games like God of War 2,
Mortal Kombat Armageddon, Bioshock and Kingdom of Hearts.

PS3 came out a few years later.
I don't remember the games I had for this one but
what made me love this system was t
he backward compatibility for PS2 games!!
Of course, I didn't have that one for very long.
Which brings me to my system I have now.

I have a Sony PlayStation 4.
Some other gamers had the XBox or XBox One consoles
which tried stacking up to The Sony PlayStation 2, 3, and 4!
They were all competing against each other for game supremacy!
Since we are on the topic of playing games...
there are other types of games
people often play that is not cool at all!

Some people can play the most childish and
petty games you could ever imagine.
Playing games with people's hearts
is definitely a big NO-NO!

It's a shame that people will play games
at the expense of others pain, feelings,
money, generosity, kindness insecurities, mistakes, etc.

God doesn't play games!
His Word is Truth and is very clear
about who He is, what He did and is doing,
what He wants us to do, and how He loves us!
Some of us are playing the wrong game.
You think you're winning but
trust me sooner or later you're gonna lose!
And my friend, it will be GAME OVER!!!

Droppin Gems

Nowadays being a gentleman is a throwback.
Being a godly person is a limited edition.
Being generic and fake is the new authenticity!
How can we solve this rapid and increasing epidemic?

Telling lies is the poison being spewed
from the lips of both men and women.
It's so toxic it can contaminate any soul.
Truth be told, watch how the drama unfolds.
The world is cruel and twisted,
no wonder we have so much grief!

Hatred has become the thief of joy.
But somehow it can never overcome
the mighty power of love.
It's no match for it!
Why can't we light a candle of compassion
in our hearts for one another?
It's so much easier to do wrong than right.
It's always a fight.
We must contend so that we might prevail.
Even if we fail,
we can continue to die trying.
Time isn't on anyone's side.
It decides what will happen and
when it will happen to us!

Jesus Take the Wheel

These problems going on these days are pollution,
let's dilute them with a potent solution.
The world mixed up in all this confusion,
people going half-crazy like they in an insane asylum.
Like En Vogue, we need to free our mind
from the incarceration of ignorance.
The key is using our cranium, class is in session...
time to learn a new curriculum.

The battle between good vs. evil
swings like a pendulum...
back and forth we go, like Star Wars
there is an imbalance in the Force!
Like the change of the tides,
we will soon see a shift in power.
Like different positions,
someone's always gotta be on top.

Life is like a movie,
throughout the duration there is a climax.
Damn, what's next?
Follow along and read between the lines...
let's not make things complicated like blurred lines.
Its loud and clear...hear and feel the noise!
Its roaring like a lion and
the feeling of anticipation is stalking you.
There is no escape.

At the end there is always silence, you fall asleep,
and you just lay there and rest easy.
You will not be disturbed...
your laying deep in a coma, you don't wake up.
You're on life support,

301

they tryin' to bring you back but
you keep slippin' in and out of consciousness.
Let's hope you come out of this one...
I can't see you like this.
Come back to life...come back to me!
Please...Jesus take the wheel!
(To be continued...)

I'm Better Off Without You

Most of the time I haven't been considered.
I never seem to ever get an honorable mention.
I'm a great and I'm in a class of my own.
I'm sexy and I'm grown.
I know my worth,
I'm the butter that makes your pancakes melt.
I should be included for breakfast, lunch, and dinner.
I thought I'd be an appetizer at least, but I
'm not even on your menu.
Its ok, everyone has different tastes.

You're a tourist and
you haven't been given a tour of me just yet.
I'm like a vacation, you should never want to leave.
Why can't you just stay a little while longer?
You should be here!
You can't handle exclusive.
Don't think I'm being intrusive.
I think you're just trying to be elusive.
I try to hide from rejection, and
I eventually become reclusive.

Now I'm trying to find my way back.
Trying to find my way back to being normal again!
At one time I thought I was, but
somehow you thought different.
Shit hits different when you feel irrelevant.
There's an elephant in the room and
damn right I'm calling it out.
Rejection is what I'm referring to
but it's for my protection.
You're not all what you're advertised to be.
You're no good for me. I'm better off without you!

303

My Plate

My plate is full. Got too much on it,
doing my best to stomach it.
But I'm bloated and overwhelmed
with so many servings life is giving me.
I enjoy buffets but I'm not a glutton. I
'm so full that I got buttons breaking off my t-shirt.
I don't have any more room for anything else
that people want to give me.
I'm at my maximum capacity so understand t
hat my load is extremely heavy.

I don't need any more sides of drama.
I've had more than enough.
A lighter plate would be sweeter than any kind of dessert.
I don't mind treating myself but I also know my limits too.
I can feed a lot of people from what's on my plate.
I'd rather bless them than to ingest them
with all the other unnecessary calories I don't need.

My strategy is to succeed and
add the right ingredients into my life.
Somewhere along the way we must learn
how much we can truly handle as individuals.
I need to eat everything on my plate that is good for me.
I can build strength from what has been given on my plate.
But sometimes what I see on my plate makes me so ill.
I would rather put my own food on my plate because
I can decide whether or not if I want to eat it or not.

Sometimes, life can serve you some things
that you were not prepared for or things you don't want to taste.
Regardless, your plate was given to you for a reason.
However, there is a chance you could be in a food coma

from everything you have on your plate.
I want to empty my plate sometimes
because I don't like regurgitating the same crap all the time.
I enjoy new plates.
But every plate has something on it.

Be grateful that you have a plate to begin with.
Whatever scraps you were given,
just remember to give God the glory!
My plate belongs to God, and I give Him my all!
My plate is enough...my plate needs to be cleaned.
Jesus once said to please take this cup from me.
I can sip from the cup, but
I ask Him to please just take this plate.
Please, LORD take my plate.

Queens Rise Up

All Queens Rise!!
We are gathered here today to celebrate you
and give you your flowers!
You reign in your respective queendoms and
rule it with an eloquence I have never seen before.
Your rise to prominence has paved the way
for your dominance of power.

Kings ruled for a time and
most of you came alongside of them
to share in that rulership.
I must say, times have sure changed!
Now you queens are holding down the court and
shifted the whole power landscape.
Queens have more authority and
are not afraid to make executive decisions.
Queens make it a priority to lead
those who are under her influence.

Queens, I love to summon your presence.
Your existence usually gives me a great experience
that I never tend to forget.
Queens you are fit to sit on the throne.
I love watching you take your place among your people.
You are kind but firm when you must be.
You are like honeybees that come from the beehive.
Your appeal stays buzzin' and
your sweetness is much sweeter than you'll ever know.

The crowns you wear have be earned and
you worked your asses off to earn that title of "Bad Bitch."
The way you walk lets me known you got confidence.
The way you speak,

echoes wisdom and enchanting pleasantries.
The way you smile brings peace to my soul.
The way you persevere in moments of challenge,
show me the type of strong leaders you are.
We love and respect you Queens!
Don't you ever forget that.
Queens, this is your time to shine and
it's time for you all to rise up!

Lazy

I feel so lazy today. I just want to sleep in.
Don't feel like getting up for work.
I don't feel like going to the gym.
I don't feel like going to church today.
I don't feel like cleaning the house either.

I think we have all had days where we
just didn't feel like doing anything whatsoever.
We all wanna chill sometimes and
most of us want to vacation somewhere.
Most of us have a pretty good work ethic,
while others don't have any gumption
to want to do anything.

Sometimes, we want things given to us
without actually having to work for it!
If we don't work, we don't eat!
Being lazy has consequences.
It can get you or someone else hurt.
Laziness is complacency and
complacency kills.
Laziness comes from your comfort zone,
and nothing ever grows from it.
Being Lazy can be a bad habit that needs to be broken.
Laziness can lead to disaster and
not lead to any good results.
Don't expect people to do things for you constantly.

Take some initiative to do things for yourself.
If you don't know how to do something
at least attempt to do it first and then ask for help!!
Laziness robs you of your blessings.
Don't be stuck in your cocoon...

at some point you must break out and
fly on your own!
Laziness can lead to entitlement and
eventually people can or will resent you for it!
So do yourself and everyone else around you a favor,
don't be lazy!

Poetry is Not Dead

If I could hold your hand,
I'd welcome my destiny.
I hope you would understand
the connection we have between us...
we're like magnets that can't help
but be attracted to one another.
I can feel your pulse...
it's in sync with my heartbeat.

Come a little closer, what is it that I see?
I see eyes that sparkle like diamonds
and the sun's rays reflecting off the ocean's waves.
Many days I've stood on the shore
watching gorgeous sunsets....
but at last, you're my sunrise that's finally arrived on time.
They say a dog is a man's best friend...
I say you're the best friend that I've ever had.

Being with you is the most fun I've ever had.
I'm so glad I found you...
God gave me a special gift to walk out of Heaven.
He sent me my own precious guardian angel...
my soul mate...my help mate.
My one of a kind...the one and only
YOU! I love you. Now and forever!
Poetry is not dead!

The Yin to My Yang

She was the yin to my yang, and I was yang to her yin.
Together, we were joined in a crazy place called earth.
A place born of sin.
It's been a pleasure to meet and
come in contact with my better half.
We didn't originate from Chinese culture, but
we are like fine China that's made with love.
We're made to last!

In Chinese Mythology, yin and yang were born
from chaos when the universe was first created.
It comes from Taoism, an ancient religion in China.
There is an ever-changing relationship between the two poles.
It is responsible for the constant flux
of the universe and life in general.
When there is too great an imbalance
between Yin and Yang, catastrophes can occur such
as floods, droughts, and plagues.

Yin and Yang are not total opposites of each other,
they are relative to one another.
Taoists believe that the universe is made up of energies, vibrations,
and matters which behave differently in different contexts.
The brake is the yin to the gas petal of yang.
The eggshell is yin and the egg inside is yang.
Yang is harder, stronger, faster, and brighter.
The yang is sunbeams, and the shadows are yin.
The pitch is yang, and the catch is yin.
Yang starts the actions, and the yin receives it, completes it.
Yin is the space inside the cup and yang is the cup.
The coffee's heat is yang and the coffee's blackness is the yin.
Yang can sometimes go berserk, and
some yins are quite powerful too!

Yin and yang balance each other out!
Nothing can ever break their inseparable bond
despite their differences!
Yin and yang are better when they are together and
show us that it's ok to be different but
unified at the same time!
What yin is to yang, yang is to yin!

Expectations

Expectations...the world is filled with various expectations.
The definition of expectation can be defined as
a "strong belief that something will happen or
be the case in the future."
It can also mean "a belief that someone will or
should achieve something."

Most of us believe we are entitled to certain things and
that we should get what we deserve.
However, life doesn't always work that way.
Your expectations shape your reality.
Life is a balance; you can reasonably expect
both good and bad of anything.
But on the other side of the coin,
life isn't always fair either.

Sometimes, we think what we invest in
will yield a great return,
but usually, it isn't always the case.
Expectations originate from hope, but
unrealistic expectations come from a selfish nature.
Most of us can say that we want more out of life.
We want everything in our lives to be better.
We focus sometimes too much on what's on the surface
rather than focusing within ourselves.
There isn't total satisfaction when
you have met your expectations because
more likely, you're never content.

Not everyone will like you or agree
with you in certain conversations.
To repair unmet expectations I offer this solution,
look inside yourself and find out

what is causing your discontentment.
Right size your expectations and
while living under the sun you can live above the sun.
Expect problems, but also expect power!
When God created us,
He expected us to love Him first...
why don't we start there.
We can expect God to be with us and
to never leave us nor forsake us!

Just Be Weird

Some people think I'm weird.
They seem to fear my uniqueness.
I just have my own style and techniques.
It's not always about finesse or
looking pretty all the time.
I know I can be a little clumsy, awkward,
and strange to some of you folks.
But hey, that's just me. Deal with it!

A lot of you idolize and revere these
celebrities, influencers, entertainers, athletes, etc.
The everyday people you see around town
become just another local schmuck.
You tend to overlook and ostracize the people you see
as a threat or whom you misjudge entirely.
You unfairly put labels on others and
put them into your little box.

I got news for you all. I'm quite eclectic and
I have an electric personality.
Most of you ladies appear to be in a state of shock
whenever you're in my presence.
My voice thunders nothing but
tender, love, and kindness.
But sometimes it rumbles
with passion and power!

I just want to be heard alright?
I want to be seen like the moon,
but not blind you like the sun.
I'm surrounded by stars cheering me on...
I've been in the sky, and you've all been
all the way down to earth.

Why are we so far apart?
I want to meet just one of you where
the sky kisses the ground...
something about this gravity of attraction
is just too strong.

It's been a long time coming.
Where do you think you're going?
Get back here and share this moment with me.
Am I too much for you?
I don't get to visit too often,
so please baby don't waste my time.
Just tell me the truth.
I embrace honesty like a close friend
especially when it comes from those sweet lips.
I salivate for a true connection with you.
There is lot at stake in this for you.

I know that's a lot to chew on.
I come with my own kind of sizzle.
I'm different. Appreciate what's in front of you.
I have everything you need.
Please don't think I'm weird for being into you.
Or better yet go ahead and think whatever you want.
I just know what I want and I go for it!
I am who I am. Hate it or love it.
If my quirks irk you, then
just go and don't let the door hit you on the way out.
When you're gone, I'll just smirk!
I knew you couldn't handle my type of weird.
I know someone out there will appreciate my kind of weird and
I'll appreciate their kind of weird.
Together we'll just be f**king weird and live a weird life.

I Don't Want to Push You Away

Sometimes, I go too far and get ahead of myself.
I can be pushy when that it's really not my intention to be.
I don't ever want to bulldoze my way into someone's life
especially when my presence isn't really welcomed to begin with.
There are times I try to be so careful, show restraint, and play it safe.
And other times, I can jump the gun, get anxious,
and rush things just a bit.

I believe I'm my own worst enemy.
I try to do the right thing but I somehow mess things up.
Things become awkward, weird, and frustrating
for the other person I try to communicate with.
I've had my share of fumbles
by saying the wrong things or
doing stupid things.
All I can do is learn, but
how many times do I have to learn the hard way.

I have flaws that I'm working on. I'm not perfect.
I can do my best to correct myself and do better.
It just seems that people hardly will forgive me
for the mistakes I do.
Sometimes, I don't have a clue about what I'm doing.
I am a work in progress and I ask for some grace.
Tears fill my eyes because I feel like people draw away from me
when I only want to get close to them.
It truly breaks my heart.

Humans are relational people but
there can be so much distance between us sometimes.
I want to close the gap.
I want to be connected like to my special someone like a bridge.
I hate burning bridges.

317

I don't like when people burn their bridges with me.
It's not easy to always look the other way
when there is an offense or an act of wrong doing.

However, we are called to love our neighbor as we love ourselves.
Sometimes I wonder, where has our compassion gone?
Whatever I've done to hurt or upset you,
I hope that you can forgive me!
I'm sorry. I mean well...I really do!
Please try to see my heart even through the darkness, pain, and hurt.
I hope we can connect again and mend fences.
I like being around you and
I hope eventually you can stand being around me too.
I just want us to do life together.
I don't want to push you away!

Shedding Off the Weight

Everywhere I go seems to be people having weight issues.
I know most of us including me would like to lose some weight.
Sometimes we need to get our weight under control.
We need a good "shred." A healthy weight makes a happy life!
Sometimes carrying excess weight can slow you down.
Like Mims, you can move if you wanna, if you wanna!
But it's hard when you got so much baggage with you.
It's time to unpack some things.
Gotta shed some light...each and every night.

I'm writing this poem to encourage us to lose some weight.
Not just physically but also mentally, emotionally,
socially, financially, and spiritually!
Most of us seem to have the weight of the world on our shoulders.
We assume we need to carry more than what we should.
Heaviness is quite a burden for one to carry alone.
You're dragging your feet because you're exhausted.
You're tired of being sick and tired.
You feel oppressed by the weight that is holding you down.

The weight of the world seems to be crushing you.
It seems to be crushing your spirit!
The weight comes with pressure, unrealistic expectations,
pain, and difficulty.
Some of us are tippin' the scales and we barely recognize it.
Brothers and sisters, it's time to shed off the weight of sin.
It's time to shed off the weight of disappointment and
discouragement. C'mon somebody!!

It's time to shed off the weight of negativity.
It's time to shed off the weight of worry, fear, and doubt.
There's no place in this life for that at all.
It's time to shed off the weight of stress and

take time to realize that we are so blessed!
It's time to shed off the weight of rejection, depression, and shame.
It's time to shed off the weight of anger and revenge.
It's time to shed off the weight of expectation.
It's time to shed off the weight of idolatry.

It's time to shed off the weight of confusion.
It's time to shed off the weight of pride.
It's time to shed off labels and walk in our rightful identity.
It's time to shed off these heavy chains.
It's time to break free and walk in freedom.
Cast aside every weight and let's carry our cross.
Our Lord and Saviors yoke is light for us.
We can cast our cares upon Him.

It's time to shed off evil forces and false prophets.
Being too heavy can make us stumble if we aren't too careful.
It's time that we shed off the weight of the past.
It's time that we should shed some tears...
it's time to shed off the weight of racism, oppression.
It's time to walk in who we are and whose we are! I
t's time we walk in our anointing!
Don't miss out on your blessing.
Don't miss your opportunity...
Go after the eternal!

God smiles upon us and most of all He loves us!
Remember, what you feed is what you lead.
I won't feed you any lies, I only speak the truth!
Nothing tastes better than the truth.
So, chew on it like you're biting a nice juicy steak!
Love is my protein, I just gotta have it no matter what.
It's time to shed off the weight of excuses and
lies and just own up to your mistakes.
It's time to put on the whole armor of God and
stand in the evil day against the evil one!

It's time to put off the old man and put on the new man.
God makes all things new.
Jesus shed all His blood for us on the cross on Calvary.
Jesus took on the weight of sin, shame, and death for us.
He suffered for our transgressions!
He made a way and I'm grateful for His love and sacrifice.
His amazing love blanketed us with sweet
compassion and overwhelming kindness.

The character of Jesus carries a great deal of weight.
We have nothing to lose when we follow him!
But don't forget to lose some weight and
at the same time wait on the LORD.
Let's keep serving Him as we continue to shed more weight!

Just Show Up

I show up for you, but you never show up for me.
I give you plenty of assists, but
you find a way to drop the ball.
Or you don't even try to take a shot!
I feel like you would rather step out of bounds
than play ball with me.
I wanted us to have a one on one.
I guess you're better off taking an "L"
on this one than being in it to win it!
I thought we could be a team.
Like Biggie, I guess it was all a dream.
I'm heated, so excuse me if I need to blow off some steam.

I made the stupid mistake of putting your ass on a pedestal!
Kept trying to get my emotions involved, but t
hey always seemed to revolve around you.
I thought we had a good chemistry...
you and I could have been the perfect solution.
The experiment failed and everything is now dissolved.
The hope of you and me is killed.
There's probably no way of coming back from that.

My pen talks but my heart is walking away from
all these troubles in my life.
I gotta find a better day.
Find a better way!
God is the only one who can show up for me
better than anyone else can.
He shows up when the sun comes out and
when the Holy Spirit comes alive inside of me!
God shows up for me because
He loves me unconditionally.
I'll keep showing up at His altar

where I can lay everything down at His feet.
I reveal my heart and He show me who He truly is!
He shows me His glory and
crowns me with unmerited favor!
I'm blessed because I showed up and
He showed out!!!

Spoken In Tears

I speak in tears,
no one can hear the pain
that I carry deep inside.
People scream all day long
about my faults and failures, but
they only carelessly whisper my achievements
or my good qualities.

People expect me to easily surrender
my rights and be labeled or put in a box.
I can't do it and nor will I ever do that.
People can't cheer for whom or what they fear.
I know you heard what I said.
I wish more hearts would be
more compassionate to cries of my soul.
The Lover of My Soul knows
His creation and only He can heal me
from this terrible pain.

Talkers, Scammers, & Hackers

I gotta get something off my brain and chest.
I've really noticed how this world is really set up.
It seems apparent to me that some people are all about
the "transactional" than the "relational."
I mean I understand that people on their hustle as am I too.
But when you get hit up from different people
simultaneously wanting $$$ it's like
hold up I'm not an ATM!
No one is entitled to anyone's money.

It's give and take...but some people do more taking
than actually giving or vice versa.
It's important to use wisdom in these matters.
People like to take your kindness for weakness.
They want something for nothing or almost nothing.
I'm not judging it's just the way I see things from my perspective.

But at the same time,
I do enjoy helping others but not to the point where I feel
that I'll be taken advantage of.
If you're gonna do business with someone,
make sure you're ethical and practical about it.
Just my take.
For the record I'm speaking to all the
telemarketers, schemers, and scam artists out there.
This isn't a shot at nobody just being clear about that!

Pushin' 40

Time keeps on slippin' into the future.
Seems like in the blink of an eye,
the years roll on by and
many changes occur in such an expansive time frame.
Our age often reminds us and others
how much older we have become.
Some age gracefully and others well...
they just get a little bit grayer on their head.
Today, I'm 37 years old, but this year I'll be 38 years old.
I'm not quite 40 just yet...
but I'm dangerously close to pushing 40!

That magic number is approaching so fast.
I'm in the twilight of my thirties.
I'm like wait a minute...where did the time go?
Time is ticking and there is still so much I must do.
But I also take comfort in knowing
that I've done a lot already.
Sometimes, I just want time to slow down.
The older you get the more you seem
to face your own mortality.
I'm still young with all things considered.
Others may view me as an "older" adult or a "seasoned vet."

Overall, I'm just thankful to be alive and it's a blessing to get older.
I'm pushin' 40, but I still look good and feel good.
I think of King David who reigned
as King of Israel for 40 years.
I also think of when Jesus himself,
fasted in the wilderness for 40 days and for 40 nights.
I even think back to how it took the Israelites 40 years
to see the promised land.

Although, I envisioned my life to be different,
I couldn't be more grateful to be where I am in life right now.
I know that the best is yet to come.
When I turn 40, I'll make sure I celebrate with a 40 ounce.
Don't be scared to be pushing' 40!
Embrace it. We can make it happen at 40.
But we don't have to wait that long,
let's get it started now.
Let's keep pushin' 40 together!!!

Trash

Everywhere you go,
no matter where it is there will always be trash.
We always must find a way to dispose of it.
One thing we all can agree on is
that trash leaves clutter and
it just leaves an unpleasant odor.

It just really stinks.
Nothing about trash smells good.
I've always heard it been said t
hat one man's trash
is another man's treasure.
Depends on your perspective lens...
trash can be recycled or dumped somewhere in a landfill.
Some people welcome trash into their lives
without ever taking it out.
A lot of times people like to dump their trash on you
and act like their shit doesn't stink.

People think toxic waste or sewage disappears but
at best all it can be is fertilizer.
Trash can be associated with many people, places, or things.
Sometimes, we'll say an athlete is trash
because of the way he or she played in a game.
We might say a certain music artist is trash
because of the song they created
was not all it cracked up to be.
We might say a movie is trash because
it wasn't what we expected it to be, or
it failed to live up to our expectations.
Sometimes, we call people trash
by the toxic behavior they exhibit.

Things that people no longer have any use for,
is all of sudden considered "trash."
Trash is clutter and it needs its own space.
I've noticed that people will treat other people like trash but
treat "material things" like pure gold.
Trash serves no purpose at all.
We can all agree that it just needs to go away
and never be seen again.

Somehow trash seems to always resurface.
Trash has been created due to mankind.
Trash in one sense can be considered vandalism
and negligence to God's creation.
At least I can see it that way.
Trash is a stockpile and needs to be isolated.
Trash is not healthy and needs its own environment!
Trash can be seen as intrusive and not welcomed.
Trash can also be a chance to sort out some things.
Trash is often seen as the lowest of the low.
Trash can be burned or buried.

But it always returns in some way.
Sometimes you can cash in on some trash.
There is a lot of trash tv that people watch.
It pollutes people's minds and
all they watch it for is for sheer entertainment.
There is nothing glorious about trash.
Filth is very unattractive.
Nothing about God's creation is trash.
However, don't act like trash.
Trash is not sexy.
Don't be trash!

Tragedy That Became a Triumph

Your lips are covered with deceit.
The lies you tell are like venom.
You're hazardous for my health.
You're attracted to wealth, power, and material things.
I gave you all I could, but
it was never enough...you wanted more!

You were starving for attention...
but only from men who were already taken.
You would rather sleep with 50 chumps and
then turn around and sleep on me.
The nerve of you girl.
I wanted you to be a part of my world
and create an empire.

But like 911, you collapsed it.
The funny thing is I'm not even mad.
I'm not gonna lie it hurt me though,
I took your best shot on the chin.
But to be honest you hit me below the belt.
But you know what I'll bounce back
and grow stronger from this.
You are now disqualified and
no longer a part of my life.
Enjoy your life being a homewrecker
since you couldn't handle making a home with me.

I wish you the best...
I let it burn and what we had is now ashes!
Gone like the wind...
what's ironic is that same wind
will push me forward to something better.
God has my back;

He'll give me way more than what you ever gave me.
So, all I can do is give you the salute and
I'll keep marching on to glory!
Remember, I'm a soldier but in the meantime,
I'll pray for you.

Reach

What are you reaching for?
That's a question we may often ask ourselves at times.
We could be reaching for an answer
to some unanswered questions.
We could be reaching for someone to talk to...
so they hear the things we haven't dared to tell anyone else.
We could be reaching for a hand to squeeze...
for some of us it may be the last
comforting touch we have before we pass on.

It may be the one thing we can hold
onto that will ever matter.
We could be reaching for love that
may not yet have arrived at its destination.
We could be reaching for the stars,
only to see them as dreams that seem so far away!
We could be trying to reach the top but
could start from the bottom or stumble on the way up.
You may even get pulled down
from those who don't want you to rise.

In basketball, I find myself reaching in to steal the ball...
sometimes it pays off and sometimes it doesn't.
In boxing, opponents are compared by their reach advantage.
A reach can be a matter of survival...
you may have to reach the shore to avoid the storm.
A reach can also be a gamble.
You win some, you lose some.
You may even be reaching down
into your pocket for something.
It could be money, your wallet,
your phone...it could be anything.

Whatever we are reaching for,
let's make sure it's worth it!
You can reach your potential by being intentional.
However, to have an effective reach
you must get in the right position.
You must know how to reach for what you want.
You won't reach everything,
but you can get pretty damn close!
Keep reaching...

You're Not Just a Number

You're not just a number.
You are counted on because
you are a part of something much bigger!
Your worth isn't defined by numbers...
its defined by love!

You are greater than any sum that is associated with you.
Your price was paid in full by Blood,
not by receipts...not by money...not by possessions!
The cross is worth more than you know.
It took One to absorb the cost.
It took One to love us all at once.
It took One to give us all hope!
It took One to give us all a future...

Wordplay

My name is Aaron and I got something to say.
It's gettin' hot up in here. Yo, somebody turn the AIR ON!
Gotta fan out those flames. Let these dames get their stare on!
Yeah, I see em' but I just see right past them.
They only see me for what I got. I'm not Sir-Simp-A-Lot.
Pimpin' is what I do. Like Lupe, this is the new cool.
I'm bridging the gaps of "This is for the lover in you"
to "This is for the cool in you!"

Put it together and you got a hot song by true R&B legends.
Yo face, on the real was the honey looking laced?
Like LL, I ask em' who do you love.
Honestly, It's not even close.
When I speak, I sometimes stumble over my words.
I had my share of fumbles in life, but
I'm one play from taking it all the way to house!
I'm winning like my name was T.D. Jakes.
My poetry can be considered a whole sermon.
Like Erick Sermon, I keep it flossin'.
I'm immaculate, I come through masculine.

I stay Ginuwine and I've been forever a bachelor!
I've been eligible ever since the NFL Draft.
Nowadays, I've declared myself single.
Most might consider me a free agent,
But, sometimes relationships can be downright flagrant.
Worse than unsportsmanlike conduct!
Like Mase and Diddy, can't nobody hold me down.
Oh no, I got to keep on moving!
None of them ain't worthy to rock my last name anyway.
There's a reason why they ain't got no ring!
Sometimes I wonder why they wanna take us under.
Why they wanna take us under!

Each stroke of my pen is like lightening.
Every word I write is a storm waiting to happen.
My thoughts have been cloudy, been felt the pain.
So now I gotta send the lyrical rain.
Like Prince, I gave you a sign of the times,
but you never could relate?
I'm from the V-town where we don't play.
Street poetry is my every day,
its real and gritty.

You can spot me in a city near you.
I'm puttin' this poetry shit on the map!
Everywhere I go I keep it all the way lit!
Like Hammer, I'm too legit to quit.
They can put me in the fire, and I'll never burn...
I'm on fire right now.
I'm blazing a trail like a pioneer.
My writing is like a souvenir,
enjoy it while it while supplies last!

Athlete

What is an athlete? According to the Oxford Dictionary, athlete is defined as "a person who is proficient in sports and other forms of physical exercise."

That is a pretty accurate definition except I would add, an athlete is also a person that competes to be the best or superior in their respective event or activity.
There is a certain level of intelligence, ability, and skill for an athlete to dominate in their sport.
I attribute a great deal of an athlete's technical prowess to their keen mental capability.
Attention to detail and being fundamentally sound can make up the difference of a natural talent.

See, talent alone is a beautiful thing, but it can only get you so far!
Leadership, preparation, discipline, focus, hustle, killer instinct, willpower, fearlessness, and intangibles can counter talent by itself.
The margin for error is razor thin and you must be willing to take some necessary risks.
Be smart, but not careless or reckless.
Play with passion but keep your emotions under control.

The way I see it, we as humans are all athletes.
We may not all have physical athletic ability, but we do have an innate desire to compete.
Majority of people like to win, and they don't like to lose.
So many expectations and pressure are put on Athletes to perform at a high level.
Stats are great, but at the end of the day it's all about wins!

That's what separates good from great!

Good athletes study their opponents and
work on their own individual weaknesses.
They pay attention to the "little things" and
work harder to improve themselves and
make their team better in the process.
It's nice to be a star athlete and all,
but if you can't lead your team to wins you fail as a leader.

Athletes should strive to be leaders and
not just be in it for fame or a paycheck.
Athletes are held to a higher standard
and mediocrity is not acceptable!
Losing should never be a mantra in an athlete's mind.
The thought of losing is like a cancer that needs to be removed
from the team, locker room, and the organization.
Losing isn't sexy.

However, on the flip side of the coin
athletes need to have good sportsmanship.
There is only one winner and in order to be the best
you have to beat the man to be the man.
Or may the best team win!
Michael Jordan is one athlete that is universally recognized as
the best basketball player of all time.
He is even considered to be the best athlete of all time.
Jordan was an ultra-competitive player and
he carries that same competitive drive
in his role as an NBA team owner.
He still wants to win, and
he stops at nothing to do all he can to win!

Part of what helps instill a winning culture is
allocating enough resources to help
bring in the right pieces to fit

your team or overall vision.
Athletes are the ones who play the game and
it's up to them to do their jobs.
The owners have their job to do as well.
Athletes should be hungry for success and
not settle for average!

I'm an athlete.
I competed in track and field while I was in high school.
The best I ever placed was 2nd in the 800-meter event.
I gave it all I had, but I didn't get first.
Sometimes you won't always win, all you can do is your best!
I'm a competitive person and I hate losing.
But I'm also a good sport even though I want to dominate!
Athletes are warriors.
They should rise to the occasion and
not back down from a challenge!
Will the real athletes please stand up?

The Ball Is in My Court

I can play any position in life.
I can drive because I go hard in the paint!
I can go left or right, cuz I know
I'll hurt feelings with my sick crossover of confidence!
I got heart like A.I. (Allen Iverson), but
yo I'm just getting warmed up!
This is just practice, we talkin' about practice.
Aye, put me in the game and watch me come off the bench
and sink it in the clutch.

My touch is finesse, I can hit from anywhere
downtown like Jordan!
I'm known for my assists, cuz
I make everything look good like Magic.
I'm a power forward, I go strong in the baseline to the rim.
Haters like to foul me, I'm like yo get off me...
don't you know I'm puttin' these monster numbers on ya?

Check yourself before you wreck yourself...
I'm Mr. Consistent, you ain't stoppin' me!
I'm out hustlin' and grabbin' these offensive rebounds
off all these aliens like Dennis Rodman!
I see my Carmen Electra in the stands,
she knows I can put that "D" on em and
dominate down low like my name was Shaq!
Here comes the boom shacka locka!
Ready or not cuz here I come, watch out for this Diesel!

I'm on fire at 3-point line like Stephen Curry...
I'm from the Bay where we don't play...
we just take it to the streets like every day...
big beats seeing ladies only...
bringin heat to em' like my name was Miami!

Like Ma$e I see you over there looking at me,
watching all the pretty things you wear...
your long hair flippin in the air make me don't care!

Girl, I want you to know, it's all love and basketball!
Baby, I'm your All-Star...
but you're no doubt my M-V-P!
Together we make a dynamic duo,
we winnin'...see us grinnin'!
Don't sleep on this superstar...
he's ready to have an unbelievable season!
Don't believe me just watch!
The ball is in my court!!

Daddy Poem

Back in the day he was a Mac Daddy
Then he became a War Daddy
Nowadays he just a Smooth Daddy!
And one day his future wife and kids
will call him Daddy.
He cruisin' in the Caddy...
they all say,
get em' Daddy!

Jack Daniels

I'm on one.
Straight off that good old Tennessee Whiskey
known as Jack Daniels.
I'm not from Tennessee but they make my favorite drink
affectionately known as JD!
My favorite drink used to be Hennessy,
but JD has taken that honor!
I love the taste and best of all the price.
JD is a whole vibe for me and yes,
I'm straight off the liquor! When I'm back outside,
I like to keep it on the rocks and stay chill.
When I'm feeling like a gentleman,

I treat myself to a Gentleman Jack.
I'm pretty sophisticated and I'm not a complicated guy at all.
I've been rockin' with JD for a good minute,
every time we get together it's always a party!
I need to go to the place JD originates from.

I graduated from Crown Royale and been off the Henny.
But Jack has been there for me
through some interesting times in my life.
I'm not saying I'm an alcoholic,
I just know what I like in a beverage!
Jack don't get you throwed too much,
but if you drink enough of them,
you'll definitely feel it that's for sure.

Stop playing with JD!
Don't sleep on Jack, it sure does know what it's doing!
Jack packs a punch and it don't slack.
JD is smooth but will sure sneak up on your ass!
Jack is straight up, and it don't play no games!

Beautiful Death

Death is knockin' at our doorstep.
It comes as a painful intruder, creeps in like a thief in the night.
Like dense fog it conceals its cruel intentions,
death never comes with an invitation.
However, we have to make our reservations
with our demise sooner or later...
death has our number, and
it seems to never to be too far away from calling us home.

The closest thing to death is sleep and sleep is the cousin of death.
Sleep is temporary and death is eternal.
There is nowhere to escape from death,
eventually we will all succumb to its dreadful presence.
In life we all make our grand entrance when we are born,
yet we make our last exit on our final curtain call.

Death has no rehearsals or auditions, it's simply a part of life.
It hurts deeply and cuts like a knife.
Death wounds us all...but as tragic as that may be,
it can also heal us at the same time.
Death doesn't have to defeat us.
Jesus eliminated the sting of death
when He was put on the cross at Calvary!
Death is not a gentleman, and it knows no chivalry,
we have our own personal rivalry with it.
But God overcame death and rose up from it,
death had no power over Him!

Death is a reward;
it gives you a chance to be reborn again!
It serves its purpose, like light and darkness.
Death will make you grieve, but
believe God sent His Holy Spirit to be a Comforter to all of us.

Death ends the suffering and torment...
just remember with death it is finished, it's done!
When it's all said and done,
we will rise again and our legacies will live on forever!
Love will reign forever...
Peace will reign forever...
His power will reign forever!
Thank God for this beautiful death!

Tired

I'm tired of being left out in the cold.
I'm tired of being left in the shadows.
I'm tired of the rain,
it keeps reminding me of the pain.
There have been times I believed
that my labor was in vain.
This struggle has drove me insane.

My wounds from each battle,
have left many stains and scars.
I go to the bar quite often
to drown my sorrows in alcohol.
I self-medicate myself with a buzz
to pretend not knowing what's real.
Sometimes, I just don't know what feel.
Other times, I just wanna say how I really feel.

People wonder how I got this way.
I got a checkered past, but
my future is like a game of chess.
Life is uncertain, yet I still keep the faith.
Even with tears in my eyes,
hope drips all over my face.
The ocean and skies are blue.
God's word is always true.
I pray day and night that my pain will disappear and
that love is restored unto me!
My heart was tired, but
my dreams are now wide awake!

Your Neck Featuring My Lips

Every chance, every glance...
I get caught up in you mesmerizing trance.
Baby, I'm in the zone and within
striking distance of my intended target.
Tonight, I'm going for your neck,
and it will be featuring my lips.
Like a vampire,
I can't wait to sink my teeth into your skin.
I want to nibble down from your neck
all the down to your spine.
Honey, you're all mine...
there is no escaping me tonight...but in these arms.
I love giving you these lucky charms.

Don't worry about anything baby,
we may set off a few alarms.
Keep calm and let the master be at work.
I enjoy breathing on your surface.
I know I'm sending chills over your body.
Bite down on these lips for me. Lick those succulent lips.
Tell me how does it feel? My tongue game is vicious.
Eyes rolling in the back of your head is so ridiculous.
I know I'm scandalous for this, but I can't help it.
You've been so anxious for my touch.
To me it doesn't seem like much to give you what you deserve.

But to you everything is everything!
My mouth waters for you.
Your neck is my lollipop.
I am addicted to your sweetness.
It's my weakness!
Kissing your neck is my fetish...it's my favorite desire!
Having you for dessert is what I require.

I admire the way you go along with my foreplay.
My flirting is very seductive.
Baby, I know you've been hurting
for me to give you the pleasures you like.
So, let me give you what you want.
Come a little closer please.
I want to leave my mark and
give you the thrill of your life. T
his poem is a track dedicated to you!!!
It's called Your Neck Featuring My Lips!

Legacy of Love

I want to be your man.
I desire to be your consistency.
You are no match for the potency of my love.

I need your intimacy,
it's all I keep ever thinking about.
It keeps me up at night.
But it's the very same thing
that gives me such pleasant dreams.

I want to make you blush with ecstasy and
make all your fantasies come true.
I want you to fancy my masculinity and
I can show you a man of full maturity.
Put aside your insecurities, have no fear my dear.
You are safe in these arms. I will shelter you from the rain,
the cold, and evil that tries to intrude upon you.
I'm your soldier. I'm assigned to you. I
t's my duty to be your defender.

Nothing about me comes disguised as a pretender.
I am a true and worthy contender
of your oh so sweet love.
I know gravity holds us both in place, but
my love will take you places you have never seen.
I'll have you reaching beyond the ceiling.
Matter of fact, I'll have you blast off
into another galaxy with my rocket launcher.
You and I can dance with the stars and
love each other to the moon and back.
I'd gladly be your morning sun...
I'd kiss you with my shining light.

Feel my warm embrace.
I'll wake you up with a beautiful
and gentle tenderness.
I got endless charm, and
I can supply you with an abundant currency
of my one of a kind love.
My love is the kind that generously gives rewards.
There are no deficits or lack of what I can do for you.
I'm a King that will sing
the praises of my hopeful Queen.
You're my present, but baby I'm your future.
Let's come together and create a legacy...
a legacy of love!

What Kind of Man Are You?

What kind of man are you?
I know that I'm a man.
An all-true man.
I always wondered what I was made of and
I found out soon enough.
I'm a man that is built tough!

So now I ask you again, what kind of man are you?

Are you a family man?
Are you a preacher man?
Are you a church man?

Are you a policeman?
Are you a fireman?
Are you a mailman?

Are you a businessman?
Are you a weatherman?
Are you a military man?

Are you the credit man?
Are you the repo man?
Are you the convict man?

Are you a surfer man?
Are you the rubberband man?
Are you the candy man?

Are you a handy man?
Are you a garbage man?
Are you a nerdy man?

Are you a hungry man?
Are you a funny man?
Are you a fighting man?

Are you a lover man?
Are you a horny man?
Are you a freaky man?

Are you a handsome man?
Are you an ugly man?
Are you a scary man?

Are you a party man?
Are you a cheap man?
Are you a broke man?

Are you a big man?
Are you a little man?
Are you a tired man?

Are you a caring man?
Are you a sensitive man?
Are you a reliable man?

Are you a gay man?
Are you a married man?
Are you a single man?

Are you a soul man?
Are you a man that leads?
Are you a man in need?

Are you a focused man?
Are you a determined man?
Are you an angry man?

Are you an ambitious man?
Are you a rich man?
Are you a poor man?

Are you an intelligent man?
Are you a man of wisdom?
Are you a passionate man?

Are you a healthy man?
Are you a sick man?
Are you a dead man?

Whatever man you claim to be is what you are.
There are different kinds of men out there.
But men also have a lot in common too.
It doesn't matter what kind of man
people think or claim you are.
All that matters is that you define
the kind of man you are now and
what kind of man you will become in the future!
Becoming a man is always an ongoing process!
Choose wisely what kind of man
you want to be remembered for!

My Muse

Your ascension has taken you on a new dimension.
If I'm your atmosphere then you're my stratosphere.
Being without you is like being without oxygen.
I'm suffocating without you...my breath is short of ambition
and I'm desperately gasping from this affliction.
Maybe, you were my addiction.

Like a •   ▪ I definitely wanted your smoke.
I know smoking is a bad habit, but
damn I sure enjoyed inhaling you.
Now I can barely exhale.
Whose gonna be there when I fall?

I am calling heaven now to find you my angel   .
I truly need to speak with you.
I guess you're in the heavenly choir
and watching over me now.
I take comfort in knowing that
your presence still surrounds me.
Oh, how I've missed your physical touch.
It's been taking a while for my brain
to wrap around the fact
that you're no longer present in the body
but present in the LORD!

I wish there was an extension for you
to be here with me a little longer.
But I can't keep you waiting for your destiny.
You've arrived to your new home...
I smile because I know I will be there soon with you.
You'll always be my muse.
Together we will be again for an eternity!

No Chill

I'm going in on this one...I ain't got no chill.
I ain't got no filter! Peeps been talkin sideways for a long time.
It's time to put this shit to rest once and for all.
These same peeps have never walked a day my shoes.
Just a bunch of bitter, jealous, and miserable people
that have nothing better to do with their lives.
I pay these idiots no mind cuz not a damn one of them pay my bills.
Not one of them has any skills to match me.

Like Ali, I'm the greatest!
The champ is here and I ain't going nowhere
so you can get to know me! I'm on top of my game.
You can't catch up to me because
I been left you haters in the dust.
See you later.
Please don't disturb, you've been kicked to the curb.

I want no remnants of you anywhere near me.
You always got your mouth open like a 7-11.
Your funky breath is foul, every word you speak is pure garbage.
The mention of your name makes me want to take a dump!
Ya'll ain't shit...You're bunch of asswipes.
Charmin don't even like your asses!
I'm gonna roll ya'll into a blunt and smoke you.
Now you've become ashes, you no longer exist.
You're in my ashtray!
I'm taking a few sips of cognac right about now.
Zero f***s given.
So, at this point you can say I got no chill!

Hitch Hiker

Once upon a time, I took a flight home f
rom Albuquerque to San Francisco.
I was coming home to surprise my mom!
On my flight to S.F.,
I sat next to these passengers who were strangers!
We struck up a conversation and
I told them about how I was taking leave
to fly home and surprise my family!
I also said I didn't have a ride
to come pick me up from the airport.
I feel bad for not remembering
any of these passengers' names...
I am so bad with names!
All I can seem to remember about them
was how kind they were to me.

As we were talking, I do recall them saying
that they were Christians.
We shared some common ground concerning our faith
which led to a powerful spiritual connection.
Then they revealed that they were missionaries.
They told me about their life changing experiences
from various countries they visited.
When we got to our destination, t
hey invited me to go "hitch-hike"
in their car en-route for me to see my mother.
It was a pretty long drive from the airport to Fairfield.
I offered to give them gas money and
I thanked them for the ride home.

While on the way to Fairfield we began talking
and I was more intrigued about missionary work.
I told the group that I was interested in becoming a missionary

and taking a trip abroad to do God's work!
They were excited for me and I was excited too!
One of the missionary leaders gave me a business card
to contact their organization called Global Passion.
I took hold of it and thanked them.

We made it to Fairfield and
we finally reached the end of the road.
All this happened circa-the year of 2013!
Fast forward seven years later
I'm going on my first international mission trip
to Colombia next month.
I believe that God prepared me for this journey
and He knew I would do His will!
Funny, it all started because of me being a hitchhiker!

My Healer

Hopes seem dashed...
praying they can somehow be resurrected.
The pain is suffocating.
Gasping for fresh air...
the mask I wear is cutting off my oxygen.
I need a breather.

Lungs were filled with so much anxiety.
I breathed in worry and exhaled doubt.
Without a doubt, I was in need of desperate healing.
Loneliness is a feeling I never wish upon no one!
Friends come and go.
But your best friend remains
the one that will never leave you nor forsake you.

His name is Jesus.
He's a constant friend indeed.
I don't have a crutch but He heals me of the sins
that have handicapped me for so long.
They were bound to leave my cripple...
but here I am standing upright in front of you all.
I've been through some things.
I've had some bad days.
I've had some good days.
But now I rejoice because He set me free!
He's a miracle worker and
He's most certainly a healer!
Forget a dope dealer...
He's, my healer!

Trouble

There is an old saying that goes,
you can go looking for trouble
or trouble can come looking for you.
Good looking out wisdom...
couldn't be any truer than that!
Trouble can run up on you anytime or anyplace.
Sometimes you can see it coming a mile away
and other times it just catches you slippin.
It's one thing to look ahead but
you gotta remember to watch your back at all times too.

Trouble is like an uninvited guest to a party.
It always wants to cause problems.
Trouble can also talk a whole lot of shit too.
It doesn't know when to stop.
Always know how to conduct yourself
when trouble comes around.
Trouble creeps on you before you know it.

I don't mean to scare you with this...
I'm just putting you on game.
Trouble is foul and it can certainly
throw anyone off their game.
Trouble can get you distracted and frustrated.
When you do find yourself in any kind of trouble,
just remember troubles don't last always.
Troubles come and go...like waves in the ocean.
Wade in the water dear children...
even God himself can trouble the water!

Mother nature likes to cause trouble in this world and
its uncertain how long she wants to stick around.
There are levels to trouble.

Steer clear of going into deep.
Don't sleep on trouble...I'm telling you that trouble
will fuck you up if you get complacent.
Trouble can strike at any moment's
notice without warning.
Trouble can make you catch cases and
lose time and money.
Trouble can get you into something
you don't want to be into in the first place.
Trouble can teach anyone a hard lesson.
Trouble loves mischief and always up to no good.

Sometimes you can go through so much trouble
to make someone feel special.
Sometimes you can go through so much trouble
to impress someone you like.
Sometimes you go through so much trouble
to get everything right.
Let's face it some people
shouldn't need to go through
so much trouble to do anything.
Leave your troubles behind and
just chill til the next episode!

No Show

I never could understand when you make plans or
some kind of arrangements with someone they are a "No Show!"
It's like how do you not even show up and
don't have the common courtesy o
f letting me know you couldn't make it!
That's pretty foul if you ask me.

Your unavailability shows that you're not a very reliable person.
Tell me what is so hard about "showing up?"
I bet you would show up if it were something
you really wanted to do or if it was at your convenience.

Being a No-Show is very inconsiderate and
it's not a good look at all for you.
A no-show tells me you don't care.
Your disappearing act isn't cute or funny.
You must think you're a ghost.

No-shows are unacceptable and
should never be tolerated.
You can't be counted on or trusted,
so you're worth none of my time.
You can't tell me nothing cuz you ain't showing me nothing.
All you had to do was show up...
now it's too late!
You're cancelled!
Now that's what you call a
"NO SHOW"

Cherry On Top

Every day I wake up trying to starve these affections of mine for you.
I've been hungry for your love all this time.
All I want is just a taste of it.
But I realize I'm not getting any of it...
so I have to fast myself from you to get you out of my system.
I wish you had some sort of craving for me.
All this good chocolate spreading around here
and it's all going to waste!
Well, that's if I choose to use it on someone else.
Maybe they will appreciate it more!
Especially, if I melt in the places, they wouldn't expect me to.

My kind love isn't what you desire...so it makes sense
you wouldn't order this fine dessert.
I don't blame you for being choosey but
I just hope you aren't being too bougie either.
My kind of flavor might just turn you out
so that could probably be why you ain't ready for none of this.
Miss me with all that bullshit...
I ain't trying to hear any of your sad excuses.
It's all good...you just have no idea what's good for you.
If you did, you wouldn't be with a bunch of these crumbs!
Oh, by the way, you forgot to have your cake and eat it too!

You have a preference and there is nothing wrong with that.
I'm an acquired taste but with the right one,
I'll be her favorite dessert like a sweet potato pie!
You could have had a slice but you were playing...
So now my next one will get every piece of me and then some!
I'll get good and plenty of her too.
While you're busy starving for attention,
me and my next will be satisfying each other's cravings.
Now, that's how you put a cherry on top!

Arrogance

Your arrogance is like the horrible stench of your ignorance.
You seem to be on Cloud nine,
I think it's time I bring you down to earth.
At birth, were you fed with a silver spoon or
did your mom drop you on your head?
I know you smelling yourself and think your shit don't stink...
but you need to know that your full of it!

You love to do things for the hell of it.
You're so selfish, careless, reckless, and irresponsible.
You have no regard for anyone else but yourself.
You're a serious head case.
You need an examination.
Pride comes before the fall.
You need to remember that.

I pray for you...I really do.
Maybe you'll have an encounter with Jesus
one day sooner or later.
Humble yourself in the sight of the LORD
and He will lift you up in due time.
You will reap what you sow!
Arrogance is like a weed that chokes itself out...that is you!
Don't be a weed. Be a seed.
Let God work through you before it's too late!

A Cup of Happy

I need something in my cup.
I need what everybody else drinkin on
that is making them smiling so damn hard.
I need whatever is making them happy.
That's it...I need a cup of happy right about now!
I've been stirred up too long...
I need a lil something to calm me down!
It's been a minute since I really was feelin' myself!
I'm not in the mood to be mad.

I wish a M.F. would!
I got a whole new vibe going on over here.
Can't get enough of them sips!
My lips are all over this good taste right now.
This is the kind of flavor I need every day in my life.
I'm tired of being sour or being around sour patches...
I'm all about keeping things extra sweet and enjoyable!
A cup of happy will do it for you,
I'm tellin' you!

Distractions

Life comes with my episodes of
drama, joys, pains, defeats, and triumphs.
But one thing that never seems to go away
are those annoying distractions.
They are like mosquitos that seek your attention
and want to suck the life right out of you.
Distractions are diversions or decoys
set up to take you away from focusing on
your tasks, goals, and dreams.
Distractions are walls that stand in front of you
to slow you down from reaching your destination or purpose.

Distractions are tricks the enemy uses
to pull you into deception!
There is a battle for our minds and whatever
we give our attention to is the master we serve!
Focus requires discipline.
It requires mental toughness and
a keen sense of attention to detail.
Distractions can leave you lost,
frustrated, lonely, and bitter.

Distractions are unwelcome intruders
that can interfere with our mental, physical,
emotional, and spiritual boundaries.
Distractions are detours that divert off
your familiar path and
take you down to an unknown road.
Distractions can lead to attacks, devastation,
constant wandering, temptations, and poverty.
Distractions can cause us at times
to lose sight of what's really important.

Sometimes, you have to tell yourself to wait a minute
and discern the intentions behind the distraction.
Anything that takes our focus off of God
is definitely considered a distraction.
Anything outside of that is an idol.
Distractions will greet you and visit you
all during the day and hours of the night.

Distractions come in many forms but
God sees through them all and
we can too with His guidance.
Sometimes, distractions are merely nothing more
than escapes that people prepare themselves to go
on during different seasons of the year.
Distractions will keep you procrastinating
and delay your time!

Distractions can also get you into trouble
if you're not careful. Distractions are the very things
you allow to rule in your life.
Don't let distractions hold power over you,
make sure you always rise above them!

Inconvenience

So many things in our existence
become inconveniences.
They come like unwelcomed visitors
that don't call to announce their arrival.
They are always unexpected and
they often lack consideration f
or our plans or schedule.
They just don't care!

Inconveniences don't seem to like
knocking like opportunities do.
They just barge into your dwelling
or space and say I'm here!
Inconveniences will disrupt
your program and
have no remorse for any of it.
Inconveniences have no consequences
to pay for their unfortunate interruptions.
They love surprises and
they think the world revolves around them.

I've learned the best way to deal with inconveniences is
to adjust and just deal with them accordingly.
You'll always have to deal with them
whether you want to or not.
Inconveniences will never apologize
for their obnoxious outbursts.
The timing is never ideal to have
a confrontation with any inconvenience.
Take its best shots and
overcome them with great endurance.
Don't let them overpower or push you around.
Stand up to them and handle them like a piece of cake!

Inconveniences won't ever be on any guest list,
remember they always wanna crash the party.
But let me remind you that
you are the life of the party.
Show inconveniences the door
after you take care of them,
then keep the party going!
I tackle my inconveniences head on.

Sometimes they can be hard
to take on all at once.
They might even slow you down.
Sometimes you have to dig deep and
find that extra strength
and be resilient through it all.
Welcome inconveniences,
they aren't meant to defeat you...
they are meant to grow you!

Landmine

Every time I have something to say to you
it could be a potential nuclear war!
Or maybe I'm just stepping on a mine field and
I could detonate your explosive anger.
Almost anything could trigger an
imminent fallout between us,
resulting in collateral damage.
Domestic violence is a ticking time bomb...
someone in the relationship or
both parties could have a very short fuse.
Diffusing a hostile situation is like
trying to crack the code to the safe.
Couples know each other's buttons to push.
People are programmed to react in certain ways...
we all have our days!
Just don't catch either one of us on one of our bad ones.

Landmines aren't easily seen or traced.
If you can avoid "landmines" I would advise you
to be cautious and be safe.
Some things however, can be so blown out
of epic proportions.
The aftermath can be catastrophic.
There could be extremely grave consequences.
Check your temperature and
don't let yourself get over heated.
But also, don't get so over heated that you mistreat or
abuse your partner.
Like GI Joe, knowing is half the battle.

Black Diamond

I'm just sittin in my room contemplating whether
or not I should do this broom challenge.
I've been thinking about jumpin' the broom
for quite some time now.
I've been trying to find one I could put on the map.
Love is hard to navigate through sometimes.

I find myself getting lost in you.
I would like to find the truth of the matter...
like why do you even love me?
I know I'm worth it...
but I have questions to which I
should probably know the answers to.
Excuse me if I need clarity.
I'm not doing any of this for charity.
My heart is more than a donation...
it's an offering. It's a gift to you!
Would you gift your heart to me?
I love being wrapped around you.

We are each other's ribbon
that ties everything together.
We can make it through any kind of weather.
Our love is prepared for all forecasts.
Nothing will ever deter us from loving one another.
We are built to last in this fast-paced world.
I'm a black diamond.
I'm not easily broken.

Do you claim me?

I've been wondering about some things lately.
My mind has so many thoughts and questions.
Some things I gotta get off my chest.
You claim that we're cool, but
it's like when you see me...
you act like you don't even know me.
WTF is that about?
You claim you got my back, but
the minute I need your assistance you bail out on me.
You claim to have love for me but yet
you hating on me behind my back.
You expect me to excuse your behavior.
Let me do all that same shit to you
and it would be a different story.
You claim to want the best for me...
but when I'm winning you ain't nowhere around to support me.
And if you're even present, you're not even clappin!

Yeah, I'm snappin...
tired of you acting like your shit don't stink!
Did you ever think as much as you need a friend,
that I need a friend too?
Tired of being left out in the cold.
Truth be told, you only seem to know I exist
whenever you want something.
I don't mind giving...but it's not cool for someone
to keep taking advantage of my kindness
or taking me for granted.
I know we all got lives but
stop acting like you got amnesia.
You ain't got dementia!
I know someone very near and dear to
me who died from that.

Don't pretend to be my friend when
You're really just a wolf in sheep's clothing.
Seems like the only time peeps wanna stake claim
is when its beneficial to them.
Some peeps are nothing more than clout chasers!
Recently, I was asked by someone
I went on a date with if I claim them.
I really didn't know how to answer that.
It's not a dig at them...but I'm thinking to myself
how can I claim someone I barely even know.
If you date someone...you can't really lay claim to them
until you put a ring on it!
When you buy something,
you are technically claiming that it is now yours...
you paid a price for the item you purchased.
If you are blood meaning you have family ties and
a member of your family doesn't claim you,
it basically means they have
denied, rejected or disowned you.

Jesus claimed all of us through His blood…
therefore, we were brought at a price.
He claimed us because He loved us
and saw value in us!
Do we love and see value in others?
Most people do...I can't speak for everyone.
The term claim seems to also carry
the stigma associated with slavery.
We are a free society.
Obviously, the cost to be free cost many lives for
the fight for freedom, but that's a different story.
We claim a lot of things in life...
but do we claim to love one another?
When you claim something or someone,
you first have to make a consideration.
You make an evaluation.

It's a careful risk assessment.
You have to vet certain people
to see if they can get access to you.
It's a process that ensures your safety and others.
Making a claim also is an investment!
Its ownership.
When I ask if you claim me,
that doesn't mean I'm handing over my rights to you.
I just want to be clear...
all I'm basically saying is
do you vouch for me?
Do you claim me?

It's Your Birthday!

I've been noticing you over there looking at me like
I was a whole snack!
I can't help if I'm a jive turkey...
but you do have good taste though!
Come over here and get you some if you dare.
I know you've been hungry for my attention.
The aroma I exude attracts and appeals to your senses!
I have everything to make you nice and full.
But wait, you're not a cannibal, right?

You're not gonna really eat me...
you just have a healthy appetite
for this hot chocolate, don't you?
I am quite nutritious like a McDonald's Happy Meal!
I just love how I make you smile.
Savor my flavor.
You can have me as a dry rub or dipped in sauce!
I'm not the type to get fried or burnt.
I'm not the roasted kind unless
you're talking about peanuts.
I'll make you go absolutely nuts!

I know you can shake and bake...make us a cake!
Please do it in a Jiffy.
We got no time to waste.
I already have the candle.
Just make a wish and I'll make it come true!
Go shorty its ya birthday!
We gonna party like it's ya birthday!

Let's Pause

I need you to take a moment
to hear my voice for a second.
Listen carefully.
I know we had some disagreements.
I know I hurt you. I didn't mean to.
You hurt me too when you made the choice
to walk out on me.
I'm not going to pretend that I will stop loving you.
No, not even for a minute.
I think you need to stop pretending
that you don't love me anymore either.
You want nothing to do with me
like I'm a stranger to you.
Love can be a strange thing at times.
I don't have it all together.
Hell, I don't even have it figured out.
I don't think I'm even supposed to.

Like music we played a sweet song while it lasted.
But like every song...they all come to a pleasant end.
I can understand if we needed to pause.
You used to tell me to practice the pause.
I realize that pausing means to listen
which also means to be silent.
Ironic how both are spelled
with the same exact letters.
Our love has been muted.
I hear nothing...
but I definitely still feel something.
I really miss your voice.
I don't want to sound like a broken record...
but can we just please practice the pause.
Baby, let's pause.

Victory

I was something like a consideration
for you at one point in time.
But for whatever reason, you decided to pass on me.
Its ok because I've got my promotion.
Emotions ran high...now
I can finally let out a sigh of relief.
Damn, it feels good to be in my position.

I've gained my acquisition.
All these years of prayer, sacrifice,
dedication, diligence, and perseverance
finally got me to this point.
I put so much of myself on the line
time and time again.
I've had some losses and gains...
but I still came out better than I was before!
I can say that I got the last laugh!

I just want to say thank you for rejecting me...
it only redirected me to someone else
who would appreciate a good man like me!
I praise God for the path and journey
He has me on right now.
None of this would be possible without Him!
I was once a nominee...
but now I'm declared a winner!
My victory came from Jesus Christ!

Let That Sink

In a world full of smooth, slick talkers...
you certainly keep fallin for the traps.
You think you know the game,
but you don't even realize you getting played!
So anxious for some attention...
you forgot to pay attention.
You want the "right one" to come along
and approach you...
but you're quick to dismiss the men
who has quality character traits.

You always get baited by these suckas!
Wonder why you can't keep a man.
You wonder why you are always hurt.
You wonder why you're always in the dirt.
You're a sucker for love...
you quick to pull off that skirt for the next guy.
You're only good for a one night stand.
I just can't stand how you think I'm a stalker...
I'm not even chasing you.
You claim you get harassed,
but you know you be giving it up like candy.

I have no agenda.
I'm just making my interest in you known.
We are adults that claim to be grown.
Communication is key. Stop trying to play victim...
you know you need to be healed of your symptoms.
Whoring around is a disease. Stop being a tease!
Stop giving out free passes.
Learn to be at ease and be still!

Open the eyes of your heart and mind to God.
Let Him show you the way.
He can turn every mess into a message!
This poem is a message to you all...
I'm serious with the pen!
Don't get it twisted...
the ink I put on paper is what I think.
Now let that sink.
So, with that being said,
let me give you a wink
for all of you who think
your shit don't stink!
Bink!

Dismissed

If you're not interested,
then why exactly should I be interested
in keeping you around?
Whatever you do is your prerogative...
but I will consider being more careful and
selective of people I choose
to enter into my circle!
I don't need to surround myself
with vultures trying to pick apart
every little morsel about me.
I'm better served if I remove myself
from people who devalue my character.

I am a man with an identity.
I know my value and
will not tolerate any disrespect!
I expect to be treated with more dignity.
So, as I pause...I realize
I'm a whole person without them.
I'm not fractured or broken...
not even losing sleep over them.
I'm awake and know what time it is.
It's time for me to move on!
Your part in my story is now over!
You are dismissed!

Dad's Still Matter

For so long dads have been so overlooked,
underrated and mistreated in our society.
I've noticed that we often have
strong affinity for our mothers
because they deliver us unto the world and
play a vital role for raising us.
That is no doubt true, but
let's set the record straight...
it takes two to create a life!
Not trying to cause any strife...
but it cuts like a knife
when fathers aren't given their due
or when they are labeled and
criticized as "dead beat dads",
unfit parents, or not a good provider in general!

It's really disheartening
when there are dads out there
really trying to be the best dad
they can be for their kids,
to only be seen as a failure as a father.
The same way we empower and encourage
our women, we need to do the same
for the men of our society.
There are some cases where most men
aren't taking the responsibility to play
the role of a father and not taking
an active interest in their children's lives.
It's not good to put all dads or
fathers in the same category.
Every man is different.

Do men make mistakes as fathers?
Sure, they do.
The same way we all make mistakes as humans.
We all can learn if we choose to make the right choice.
Fathers truly make a difference and
can bring stability and structure to the family dynamic.
Some single parents handle a dual role and
that may not have been what they wanted but
that is the reality we face today.
Fathers are called upon to be the
spiritual leaders in their household.

A father's voice and actions
serve as a catalyst for their child.
It assures them of their love,
affection, protection, and devotion.
Don't be so quick to dismiss fathers
like they don't matter...please believe that
DAD'S STILL MATTER!!!

1st Place to the Last Place

There is so many people fighting
to get 1st place in your life.
Yet there is only so much of you
that you can give to anyone.
Sometimes, people have to wait and be patient.
Their time will come or maybe not.
But there is always room for improvement.
I apologize if anyone has ever felt like
I left them in the basement.
I'm just a man on this earth with an assignment.

If I had it all I would give it all back to those I love.
But keep in mind, there is only one person that will ever
get all of me...that person is my God!
He is my first love because He loved me first
before anyone else ever did!
I'm not feeling guilty with the divine appointment
I made with the Creator.
You better believe I gave Him 1st place.
Like Prince,
I won't let the elevator bring me down...oh no, let's go!
You ever heard of elevation requires separation?
I'm in preparation to ascend and
be with my Father who art in heaven!

Don't be offended, I'm only human.
I'm a man that lives in a broken world
just like the rest of you.
Your perception of me isn't gospel...
just merely a speculative opinion.
Just understand one thing I'm a man of God...
I got dominion to trample over serpents and scorpions!
I can do all things through Christ who strengthens me.

I worship my God in spirit and in truth!
If you want to be with me, follow Him.
If not, I'll understand but I'll pray for you.

I hope for lost souls to find their way back home.
Step out of the darkness
into the marvelous light of glory.
I want you all to have what I have.
Let us all be joined together
like the 206 bones in the human body!
Many of us have skeletons in the closet...
have no fear, bury the bones of the past.
Let them be resurrected like
Jesus when He rose on the 3rd day.
Let those dry bones raise up and
live like the ones in Ezekiel!
Speak life to your bones...
whatever is dead let it be dead.

But what remains shall be everlasting!
Old things pass away, but all things become new!
Be new creatures and receive your crown.
Leave your frown behind and
make a joyful noise unto our King!
Let heaven and nature sing
the glorious name of Jesus!
We were all born into the world, but
now we are all here together in the heavenly skies
praising the Holy of Holies!
We have become reconciled to our Father.
The earth was a temporary holding area and
we tried to be 1st place in it.
Heaven is the last place we go and
it's the best place we could ever be.
Thank God for our new home!

A Passenger Becomes a Messenger

I remember growing up I lived on a street called
7 Buss Street in Vallejo, CA.
I was notorious for always catching a bus
going to school or anywhere else in town.
I also grew up on another street known as Florida street.
Which is funny, because
I currently live in the state of Florida!
It's ironic that these signs both ran parallel and
are relevant to my present state.

So anyway, let me introduce you to my story.
I've been waiting at the bus stop.
I wait patiently to get a ride to a destination called home.
From a faraway distance
I begin to see lights approaching me.
It appears like my light at the end of a tunnel.
It's been a dark path for me...
it seemed like I couldn't see past another day.
So, these lights I see are from a bus that
I've been expecting for a while now.
The bus comes close to my stop, but
much to my disappointment...it drives right past me.

At this point, I am devastated.
Life can be like that sometimes.
It doesn't cooperate on our time schedule...
we have to adjust on its time.
Life has a way of letting you know
when it's time to do something or
when not to do something.
Or it could just be something delayed,
but it doesn't mean it's denied.
I have conversations with God

waiting for some kind of reply.
Sometimes I get impatient
wanting instant results
or instant gratification.

I'm learning that I need to let
patience have her perfect work.
Trials will come.
Storms will come.
Trouble will come.
I know I will suffer some consequences.
I will endure the afflictions.
I will run my race of persecution.
His strength is more than sufficient
enough for me even in my weakness.

I've missed a few buses.
I've had my share of disappointments.
I've had my share of losses.
I've been hit hard many times.
I've even fell a few times too!
I still continued on in spite of it all.

I may not be noticed by everyone...
but I know who's always watching
and applauding me.
He is the one who had written all my chapters
and He knows my next one.

Faith is the evidence of things not seen.
Yet in the midst of my journey,
I can sense God's presence all around me.
His unfailing and endless love always surrounds me.
When I am down to nothing...
my LORD God is always up to something.
One day I will take my last ride.

It won't be on a 🚌.
It won't even be in a car. It will be in a coffin.
My body will be present,
but my Spirit will be with the LORD.
When I take that last precious breath...
you know where I'll be.

There won't be any more bus stops...
pit stops...or even hospital visits.
I'll ascend to glorification...
a place we know as Heaven!
I'll be known as a passenger
that became a messenger!

We See You

Ladies, we see you from a distance and
appreciate the view even more up close.
Men are curious creatures especially
when we lay eyes on those exotic features.
We are drawn to examine and study
the fascinating curriculum
of this wonderful attraction.

You deserve more than
just a fraction of my attention.
I'm focused on you like solar system.
I'm glad to say I've made an amazing discovery.
You're like my favorite TV channel
that I'm seriously into watching.
I could always go back to this episode
over and over in my mind again and again!
Ladies, we definitely see you!

From Walls to a Foundation of Love

You build walls that are monuments of nothing.
What were you hoping to accomplish?
Trying to keep me from getting over to you, I'm sure.
I suppose you can build a wall...
but why spend all that time and
labor doing that when you could just put up a fence.
At least we can talk like civilized adults
while still keeping up a boundary.

You lay bricks, but you're laying them
for the wrong foundation.
We were supposed to build a house of love.
We needed cement and there was no more
to put on our bricks.
We needed something that was
strong enough to stick.
Love would have been the right solution.
Love is the cement.
It takes hard work to make cement.

It's easy to quit and stop working on the foundation...
I learned that a relationship is a labor of love.
If love has value,
why on earth would we throw it all away?
Sure, we will have our storms,
disasters, and not so good days...
but that is what strengthens love.
Its ok to fall sometimes, but it's not cool to stay down.

I'm trying to build an empire and a fortress
that can withstand any force that comes against it!
I want to build that with you as my queen.
We aren't meant to do life alone.

I don't mean to sound like I'm getting attached,
but I'm not Leggos...I'm not a detachment.
I'm an enhancement.

You are too baby. We are made to heal and that's real!
I know I've been sweating you over some stupid things
and I'm sorry about that. I just care so much about you.
Truth is I really don't know what I'm doing.
I'm doing my best. I just need a little help from my friend...
my best friend....YOU!
I wanna see what we are made of!
I don't want us to build barriers against each other.
If anything, let's build a bridge called love.

I'm not ready for a collapse...let's rebuild like
The World Trade Center Memorial Towers.
We can rebuild our structure
from the ground up and focus on our future.
May God be the center of our house of love.
May He be the roof. I'll be the pillars and insulation.
You can be the decoration, joy, peace, love,
and warmth to this house we build!
Let's vow that on this day as for me and
our house we will worship the LORD at all times!!!
Emmanuel is with us.
I love you. Amen!

Be My Lady, Not My Mama

I need you to be my lady, not my Mama.
I don't need the drama, ok?
I know I probably cause it sometimes and
I'm sorry but what I don't need
is the extra drama in my life right now.
I'm a full-grown ass man...
I'm capable of taking care of my own self.
I know you mean well and you're a caring,
loving, and nurturing person, but
sometimes you be doing too much!
I love you but on the real
you can get on my nerves sometimes.
I know I get on your nerves too.

My mama helped raised me to be the man I am today.
The man that is with you is by far not perfect but
he's striving to be the best man he can be.
I admit, I do need a bit of help sometimes
and I know I can be prideful.
I had to learn to swallow it and
be honest with the man in the mirror.
But you are the better half of me in the reflection.
I know you're protective of me as I am of you.
I love, admire, and adore you for who you are.
We all make mistakes and sometimes
we need to just learn and grow.
I know you're a multi-tasker and
you like to correct things that seem out of order.
But with all due respect...
be my lady, not my mama!

By Now

Once upon a time I was told
all things come to those who wait.
Like a fisherman, I'm still hoping to get my catch.
Patience is preached but seldom ever practiced.
Life does what it wants,
we just go along for the ride.
All we can do is hold on and
weather the passing storms.
Sometimes I think this too shall pass.
By now my time should have come.
By now I should have received my blessing.
By now I should be winning.

I learned that life is a marathon not a sprint.
Not everything happens in the blink of an eye.
When you go the distance expect to meet resistance.
Resilience is a form of brilliance...
therefore form an alliance with it.
By now my prayers should have been answered.
By now I should have experienced everything I wanted to see
and do in my season under the sun.

So, what gives?
Well, I had to learn how to dance in the rain.
I can stand the rain because it made me grow
from all the pain I had to endure.
I should know where I am in life
and where I'm going by now...
sometimes I feel lost in the shuffle like a deck of cards.
Like a king with an ace up his sleeve,
I should be on top of my game.
I could be the jack of all trades
with a royal queen to rule by my side.

I realize I have a heart of gold,
but this cold world is full of jokers.
I call it like I see it...a spade is a spade.
A club is a club...and a diamond is a diamond.
I should know my odds. Opportunities are few.
All I need is a chance to capitalize.
I've fantasized about success and
reaching the top of the mountain.
Yet somewhere along the way,
I realized the number of steps it took
to get me where I am now.

It's quite remarkable.
By now I thought I would have fallen.
By now I thought I would lose.
By now I thought I would be dead.
By His amazing grace, I'm still here.
By now and by faith,
He has been with me all this time.
I'm blessed and so grateful for His love.
It took me a long time,
but it took Him revealing who He was
to finally get my attention by now.
I was blind, but now I see...
I'm a witness, seek and you shall find.
If you don't get it by now,
eventually you will...keep living!

Quitting

Sometimes, I feel like I'm the only one on my own team.
I do all I can to encourage myself to keep trying...
to keep going...to keep believing...to keep praying.
But it sucks when you have no one cheering
or supporting you on the sidelines.
I feel like quitting.

Seriously, I really do.
I struggle in almost every
area of my life and I'm just tired.
I've put in so much effort and
I've always been determined to succeed.
Yet I'm always failing.
Nothing I do seems to even matter.
So why even bother?
I don't mean to have this attitude,
it's just where I am in my life.
If you all can even understand that.

I am often misunderstood by so many people...
they just don't get me.
I don't have time to explain myself.
All I know is somebody better come get me
before I lose myself.
Life is insane most of the time and
I'm doing my best to keep my sanity.
It's easy for people to sit back and judge but
you never walked a mile in my shoes.
I know I'm going places,
but sometimes I just get stuck.
I always feel like in life
you are assigned to carry so many things.
I really just want to drop it and lay it all at His feet.

I can only do so much.
What do people want from me?
What do they want from me when
they don't even like having me around?
Grace and mercy abound all around me from God...
but where is it from people near or far?
I feel broken. I feel weak. I feel weary.
I'm hurting. I feel like I'm losing.
God, I send my S.O.S. and right now I surrender.
I need you Lord cuz
I'm about done with all this suffering!
I'm thinking about quitting!

Fallen Kings

We have some fallen kings in our midst
my brothers and sisters!
Nothing is promised in this life except
death and taxes like Benjamin Franklin once said.
Death is our reward and we give back our lives to our Maker.
Many kings have fallen by natural causes, by the sword,
by the gun, by sickness, or by the hands of a woman!

I want to give a moment of silence to our great kings
that have passed on.
Let us honor our Kings and
give them more than their flowers.
Kings, we need to pay homage to
the late, great Dr. Martin Luther King Jr.
He is a hero and icon for all American people.
He changed history for the better and his legacy lives on!

Malcolm X was controversial,
but he fought to make change
and bring equality for black people.
He did this by any means necessary!

Muhammad Ali was known as "The Greatest."
He moved like a butterfly and stung like a bee.
He was a man of conviction and
considered by many a legend and
icon in the black community.

As I'm honoring these Kings,
there seems to be no immunity
from the tears that fall down my face.
Every King I mentioned has meant something
in a profound way to black people.

The list goes on.
Kings like Nelson Mandela, Otis Redding, Sam Cooke,
Frankie Lymon, Marvin Gaye, Maurice White, Eazy-E,
Tupac Shakur, Christopher Wallace, Emmett Till,
Trayvon Martin, Oscar Grant, George Floyd,
Philando Castile, Young Dolph,
Nipsey Hussle and Ahmad Arbery, and Kobe Bryant
were all gone too soon.

All these men died tragically but
they left us with some great lasting memories.
One of my biggest inspirations I lost in my life
was my late grandfather aka Papa.
I learned a great deal from him and
he taught me how to be a man and
have a strong work ethic
he loves just as hard as he worked too,
I love and miss him dearly, he's definitely a king!

My baby brother, Casey Sean Rodriguez
your life ended just before it began prematurely.
God took you back home, but no matter what
you're still a king in Big Brother's eyes.
Love you little bro.

To all my other kings, I want to honor you as well.
Bruce Lee and Brandon Lee,
you both left an incredible legacy for the world.
You still kick ass. Rest in peace Kings!

Bob Marley you are a legendary King of Reggae and
your music lives and brings healing
to all people around the world.
James Brown you're the
Godfather of Soul, Rest well King!
Elvis Presley you definitely were the King

and showed the world how to rock!
Your impact is extraordinary, Rest in peace King!

Little Richard you're the King of Rock and Roll, rest well King!
Jimi Hendrix you were killing it on that guitar.
You were untouchable, rest well King!
JFK thank you for being a stand-up president.
Respect to you King!
Colin Powell, you are a general, soldier, and
a major political figure.
Salute to you King!
John Lewis you were a civil rights trailblazer
and you left no doubt left an indelible legacy.
You are missed King!

Bernard Tyson aka Mr. CEO of Kaiser Permanente
you are such a titan and provided so much for the Healthcare
Community. You are the People's Champ!
You are family and we lost a great man.
You're gone but certainly never forgotten,
rest in power King!

Uncle Ernie I had only one chance to meet you.
But you were so loved and cherished.
I followed in your footsteps as you were a
United States Air Force veteran.
Thank you for your service and having a heart of gold.
Love you Unc, till we meet again. Rest in peace.

Smoking "Joe" Frazier, Marvelous Marvin Hagler,
Arturo Gotti, Kimbo Slice, Hector Camacho Jr, Johnny Tapia,
Big L, Big Pun, DJ Kay Slay, Ol' Dirty Bastard,
Jam Master Jay, Nate Dogg, Prodigy,
Biz Markie, Heavy D, Andre Harrell, Craig Mack,
Black Rob, and Shock G we miss all you great Kings!

Mac Dre, we miss you out here in the Bay Area.
We still do that Thizzle Dance in your memory.
Coolio we'll see you in Gangsta's Paradise.
John Singleton you're a pioneer in the film industry
and gave us many Hood Classics like
Boyz in the Hood and Higher Learning to name a few.
Rest in peace King!

Sidney Poitier, you were the first black man to win an Oscar.
You paved the way for so many future kings like
Denzel Washington, Samuel L. Jackson, and Morgan Freeman.
Much respect and love king. Rest in peace!
Chadwick Boseman, you were our champion and black superhero.
Losing you was a great blow,
but now you can rest well knowing that it's Wakanda Forever!

Bernie Mac, I tried to tell her about those
milk and cookies and I said him downstairs! LOL.
You truly were a king of comedy and you've always been a funny
MF! All love king, rest in peace!
DMX the dog of all dogs, you were a force to be reckoned with
in the rap game. You're the grand champion we miss you
Rough Rider, rest in peace X! Grrr....

Brigadier General Charles McGee, oldest Survivor of
Tuskegee Airmen salute to you and your service.
Thank you, king, rest in peace!
Kevin Samuels, you were a scholar,
but often misunderstood.
You were a strong voice for black men, and
I appreciate you for standing up for us.
Rest in power king!

Lastly, I want to honor these two kings that left us much too soon,
Prince Nelson Rogers and Michael Joseph Jackson.
Two of the arguably best musical artists the world has ever known.

I grew up listening to their ingenious and life-changing music.
I still listen to their jams to this very day.
I was truly hurt when these two kings passed on.
They both were often compared to each other,
but they were neck and neck on the talent spectrum.

MJ was known as the King of Pop and Prince was known...well as
Prince! However, MJ and Prince were pretty equal,
and they influenced a whole generation.
They both are Kings, and both will go down as the best to ever do it!
For now, we say farewell and pay our respects to these great kings as
they have all ascended to a higher calling... Heaven!
We love and miss them dearly.
Every king that is no longer with us, just remember we hold you in
high regard and honor you for being the king that you are!
Rest in peace my Kings and God bless all of you!

The Power of Positivity

Ladies and gentlemen,
I don't know if anyone's ever heard that
there is power in positivity.
This world needs and craves it more than ever!
Positivity is longevity.

When we engage in positive activities
something remarkable truly happens…
we actually feel good!
There is nothing like positivity.
It's good for our health, well-being, and
most importantly our souls!
Positivity fills the space with abundance.
Positivity encourages, inspires, and
delivers kindness every single chance it gets!
I embrace positivity like a warm hug and
I shrug off negativity that tries to creep up on me!

Positivity is like a kiss of joy.
Positivity is like a sweet aroma
of a cake baking in the oven.
But wait a minute, the best part of positivity
is the icing on the cake!
Positivity is a recommended prescription
to the issues plaguing this world today.
Positivity truly makes all the difference.
Receive positivity.
Bless others with positivity.
Positivity surrounds us all,
just don't forget to plug into
the power of positivity.

Double Standards

You ever feel like there are rules that people don't follow
and they expect you to follow them?
Sounds hypocritical, doesn't it?
Another example is
when it seems the rules don't apply to certain people or
a group, but the other people want to hold you to them.
It's like they are ready to condemn you and hold you to the fire.

This is what is known as double standards.
Men and women deal with this problem very frequently.
People that are leaders or tasked with responsibility of leading others
will often abuse power and try to rule with an iron fist.
It's one thing to hold people accountable, but when you're not
accountable there is a big problem with that.
It creates controversy, discord, confusion and resentment.
There is a popular saying that goes,
"Do as I say and not as I do!"
Sounds familiar, right?

Double standards are very contradictory in general.
I really despise double standards and
most people feel the exact same way that I do.
One double standard I really don't like is
when women express their emotions
that they can use it as an excuse of being emotional,
but a guy can't really express himself by being emotional
because he's viewed as violent, creepy, or weak.

In other words, most women tend to get rewarded or
exonerated for poor behavior while
men get punished for expressing any kind of emotion.
Women experience double standards just as much.
For example, most women are expected to cook, clean,

and look after the household while
men don't have to do those things except work.

Another example is that most women get paid significantly
less than their male counterparts in the workplace.
Or that there shouldn't be any woman working
in a male dominated field of expertise.
Double standards are basically tired ideologies
about gender roles, and they should not ever be
tolerated or allowed to occur!
If there is to be equality,
then double standards need to be ruled completely out!

Meant Nothing to You

Be honest...I never meant anything to you!
Like c'mon you know and I know
I never meant anything to you!
It's a hard pill to swallow when I realized
I meant nothing to the person that meant a lot to me.
Life can sometimes offer up some bittersweet moments.
To look in your expressionless eyes tells me everything.

It's like I see a ghost.
There is no warmth...no compassion.
Not so much as even a morsel of remorse!
This whole thing between you and I
have run its course.
Everything is so dry now.
There isn't a drip of care that you leak out of your soul.
Your heart is frozen like a tundra.

How can you be so cold?
I did everything I could do for you and for us.
For you to act this way really tells me a lot about you.
I know sometimes things are not meant to be...
But that doesn't mean you should act like
I meant nothing to you!! I'm not garbage.
I still clean up nice and still hold down my position!
WTF is your problem?
You probably won't even say because
I remember that I never meant nothing to you!

Swan Song

I'm sure we've all heard the fairy tale of the ugly duckling
that turned into a beautiful, gorgeous swan!
Can't love the lovely if you can't embrace the ugly.
Similar story of the caterpillar turning into a butterfly.
Nature takes its course for changes to occur.
To some people you'll be the ugly duckling,
but to other people you'll be viewed as a swan.
Both the ugly duckling and swan have one thing in common.
They are both birds that are made for the water.
I know that I'm not made for it, because I don't swim.

Watching them both glide downstream
is something like a dream.
The past reflects who you used to be.
But when you stick out your neck and dare to grow,
you become like the swan of your future.

The ugly duckling reminds me of the struggle
I endured and the time.
The swan is what I'm becoming, but
once I spread my wings I'll really begin to soar.
Swans are graceful and they really know how to move.
It's been said that swans sing one beautiful song
just before they die.
Swans don't actually sing
but they do hiss and snort.

However, before I die, I hope to find my swan mate.
Swans are known for their loyalty to each other.
Two swans swimming with their necks intertwined
in the shape of a heart is a universal symbol of love.
One day we will all have our swan song!
What will yours be?

www.ingramcontent.com/pod-product-compliance
Lightning Source LLC
Chambersburg PA
CBHW070900120626
46546CB00001B/73